A PROMISE MADE

IN PURSUIT OF THE IRON DREAM

By Shad Ireland

DEDICATED TO

This book is dedicated
to my family, friends, and
supporters. We still have
miles left to go and choices
yet to make. And to those
patients who I hope to inspire
with my experiences; I would
encourage you to remember
who you wanted to be.

THANKS TO

To Shelly, LaVone, Tobie, and John, at Voila! Media Group; I could not have done it with out the four of you. You shared my dedication and commitment to helping others and continued to support me and my foundation as we struggled through the first year. I really value the relationship we have developed and consider all of you great friends. Thank you for believing in me. You do such amazing work.

To Karen,
You were there in the beginning and supported me when things got tough. You were there when others left. Your friendship and support helped me to achieve what many said could not be done. Thanks for Lance's book. It helped me get through the rough times.

To everyone I recognize in Mile 8 of this book. Your relationships have been invaluable to me and continue to enrich my life. I have learned so much from all of your experiences, and each of you will continue to remain a source of personal inspiration.

MILE MARKERS

INTRODUCTION

It is amazing to me, to think about how one event in someone's life can inspire and change that individual and also dramatically impact so many others. The Ironman World Championship was that event for me. It was the catalyst that inspired a promise to be made, and not only did it change my life, but it has helped to shape what has become a pivotal belief system that made me the Ironman that I am today.

It was the end of March back in 1993, and here in Minneapolis, The University of Minnesota Hospital became the setting for six weeks of what would become a life altering experience for me. It was there that I wound up in a coma battling for my life. I had been diagnosed with a pseudo tumor (brain) ARDS (Associated Respiratory Distress Syndrome) and was in the process of a full blown rejection episode. I was losing my first kidney transplant and went from 145 lbs to 75 lbs, with the doctors telling my family that I would not make it through the next 24 hours. To everyone's surprise and amazement I came out of the coma and was discharged a couple of weeks later to my mother's house to recover. I spent the next 13 months on her couch and that is where it all began.

I can't remember if I was watching the race itself or a story about these amazing athletes, triathletes they were called, but I do remember these athletes were competing in an event called the Ironman located in Hawaii. I was mesmerized by, and in awe of these athletes; the impossibility of the race itself seemed to draw me in. It consisted of a 2.4 mile swim, 112 mile bike ride and a 26.2 mile run which needed to be completed consecutively. As I watched, transfixed by what I was seeing, I began to ask myself as these amazing athletes crossed the finish line, "How can they do that?"

A giant grin came across my face as I laid there watching, weighing a whopping 75lbs! The wheels started to turn and I thought to myself, "I can do that." I promised myself that would be me one day, running with the best athletes in the world. A life changing promise was made that afternoon and the impact of that promise would one day affect not only me, but many other kidney dialysis patients, their families and family members, and even healthy individuals from all around the world.

Eventually I recovered, and got back to dealing with my life. It had been many years since I made that promise to myself. It was all but forgotten, and then a fateful late night conversation with a couple of friends triggered the memory of those dark events back in March of 1993.

I sat there in a state of retrospective remembrance, and just as it had so many years before, slowly, that same grin crept across my face. I remembered a promise made and I boldly stated to my friends that I was going to compete in the Ironman World Championship! I am telling you this because a promise made changed my life. One event, one pursuit, the Iron Dream. That same grin I told you about earlier is on my face right now as I write this and think back to when it all started and how the Ironman set all of this in motion.

Friends, this is my story.

MILE 1
IN THE BEGINNING

The race for my life began in May of 1983....

May is such a beautiful month. The smell of spring fills the air. Everything is alive again and the beauty of new life is everywhere. I've always loved May. I was born then. In 1983, I was ten years old and looking forward to being eleven. It was only two weeks away, and like any ten-year-old child I was filled with energy and excitement. Unfortunately May 13th was the day my childhood ended and that energy and excitement soon changed to uncertainty and fear. That young, beautiful, spring afternoon became the day I was forced to grow up and face the reality of my existence. I will always recall May 13th, as the day that I was told a part of me had died.

I remember it all so clearly. The door opened slowly and the doctor entered the room. He took a position of authority, never sitting down. From where I was seated he seemed like a giant that towered over my mother and me. He began to talk to her and as he did it felt like a dark cloud filled the room. After awhile he bent down and his hand touched my knee. "Shad, I need to explain something important to you." I began to shake like a child who was about to be punished. The doctor proceeded with a stoic tone that never wavered. "Your kidneys are sick. They are having trouble doing their job and they need some help." I became very quiet and looked up at my mother for reassurance, holding onto her arm. What I saw was not the reassurance I needed. Instead I looked at her and watched as tears filled her eyes.

My mind was racing. All I could focus on was my mother and her tears. Why is she crying? I don't feel that sick. I could hear the doctor's voice muffled in the background of my thoughts, but I was not paying attention. Then I caught the tail end of the conversation between them. He proceeded to explain the process that we would need to follow and as he spoke, I could see that he scribbled on paper two prescriptions. One was to correlate with a procedure called a kidney biopsy that was to be done within the next week at Children's Hospital. The other was for a drug called Prednisone.

After leaving the Doctor's Office, we went to the pharmacy to get the prescription for Prednisone filled and as we walked out to the car the dark cloud that followed us along proceeded to bring the rain. It was not a typical rain. It was a cold, wet, spring-like rain. They were big, heavy raindrops that looked like children's marbles. The smell of fresh wet blacktop filled my nostrils as I stood there, getting soaked waiting for my mother to unlock the car doors. The ride home seemed wrong. I felt like something needed to be said, but my mother was in a world of her own, the silence broken only every three seconds by the urgent swish of the wiper-blades across the glass, as those big heavy raindrops turned into a down pour.

Several weeks would pass before we could get an appointment to perform the biopsy, and as each one went by my kidneys continued to fail. My body began to swell and I started to retain fluid. I would wake up in the morning and my eyes would almost be swollen shut. I would look in the mirror and barely recognize myself. By noon the fluid that had originally gathered in my face had moved to my legs and it hurt to walk. I could take my thumb and push the skin all the way to the bone leaving a deep indentation that would last several minutes. Each day that went by brought new struggles and new symptoms. I had a permanent headache which I would find out later was caused from having high blood pressure (A side effect of my kidney failure) and every time I ate I became violently ill.

My days seemed to drag and my nights were filled with short periods of sleep followed by what seemed like hours and hours of dark silence. The constant pounding in my head kept pace with my thoughts, both causing severe pain and fear. Finally it reached a point where because of the fluid building up in my body, sleeping lying down was impossible. I went from using one pillow, to two pillows, and soon I needed three. If I was lucky a good night meant MAYBE two hours of sleep. When I couldn't, I used to get up and wander around the house. I remember how quiet it used to be. The one noticeable sound, being the movement of the clock hanging on the wall. Every sixty seconds you could hear the big hand click into place. Some nights, I would sit and stare at that clock for hours. With just the sound of my fearful and frantic thoughts, coming in waves, crashing against the shoreline of my mind, and the precise movement, every sixty seconds keeping me company. The nights eventually turned into mornings. I think it was some time between the six and the seven that I developed a need for constant chatter. But it was that constant chatter that distracted me from the hurricane just on the horizon. It's funny, many who know me believe that I love to hear the sound of my own voice, and to be honest, I have through all of this, developed a fondness for the symphony of sentences that played throughout any given day.

It was never easy for me, and so there were times when I would embrace the cool kiss of the bathroom floor tile. The sick feelings would be so strong, that I would spend minutes with my head almost in the toilet bowl repeatedly flushing so I could feel the refreshing mist of the clean water as it sprayed against my face and bounced off the white porcelain. Contained within these minutes I saw what I thought would be my future as I watched the water spiral and disappear.

Then the day finally came for me to go to Children's Hospital and have my kidney biopsy that Dr. Veneer was to perform. After introducing himself he began to explain the procedure but all I heard was blah, blah, blah (Twenty minutes earlier the nurse had come into my room and given me a shot which helped to prepare me for what would be the first of many intrusive experiences).

I don't remember having the kidney biopsy, but what I will never forget is what they told me had happened during the procedure. Apparently I struggled to get free, biting on someone's arm and punching Dr. Veneer in the face. It took several people to hold me down and a large dose of sedatives before they could proceed.

Dr. Veneer was an older man who smiled a lot when he spoke and often reminded me of my grandfather after he'd had a few beers. So as I laid there I found my thoughts began to drift to a much earlier time, a time before I became sick.

Grandpa Ireland was an alcoholic. So much so, that all of my memories involve him consuming some sort of alcoholic beverage. I will always remember his smell. His favorite cologne was a cheap brand called beer. Both of my parents were nurses so while they worked Grandpa Ireland would baby-sit my brother and me. One night he decided that he wanted to go to the corner bar that happened to be six blocks away. He took my brother and myself (ages seven and four at the time), to what I thought was an amazing place. I remember people laughing and music playing. The best part was that my brother and I got to eat lots of hot french fries and all the orange soda pop we could drink. Eventually the night came to an end and my brother and I found ourselves pulling a little red wagon which contained our grandfather who was too drunk to function. We pulled him all the way home and when we arrived our mother who was frantic and furious greeted us. She had finished working a double shift and arrived home to an empty house. I remember her screaming, "Richard Ireland, what are you doing?" and Grandpa Ireland replied, "Babysitting".

The next several weeks went by painfully and slowly as we waited for the results of the kidney biopsy. I vividly remember the day they discharged me from Children's Hospital. They told my mother there was no need for me to stay any longer and that there was nothing that could be done until they had the biopsy results. So they carried me from the hospital bed to a wheelchair and out to my mom's car. Then they lifted me from the wheelchair and put me into the front passenger seat. Without hesitation I laid down and began to wretch and vomit profusely. So there I was lying on the front seat of the car holding a large basin half filled with puke. My head was pounding and tears filled my eyes as panic set in. I begged and pleaded, wanting to stay. I could not understand why they were sending me home. I felt like I was going to die. I wanted to scream, "Why won't you help me?" but I couldn't because my mouth was filled with vomit. My mom started the car and began to drive. As we headed home, she placed her hand on my head and told me that everything would be all right... but I knew she was really choking back the tears.

The rapid onset of my disease was rare and initially confounding. So much so that the anticipation was quite high as everyone waited for the kidney biopsy results. Those results would allow my doctors to see exactly what they were dealing with and would provide the diagnosis and hopefully some answers that would lead to a treatment plan. Unfortunately the answers we wanted, would only lead to more questions, questions that could only be dealt with in time.

As individuals, there are always certain pivotal points that will change the direction of our lives forever. It's at these points where we always seem to universally find the answers. It's where all of the punch lines to life's jokes finally make sense. For me, it's like the last page was written long before the first page was read. But it is from within these previous pages that I was able to begin to change from who I had become with kidney disease, to who I am today.

That rainy spring day back in 1983 was the first of those previous pages. You see, it was the day that I asked that one question of myself: "Why did this happen?" There are three concepts that gave me the answers to that one question that I've asked myself for the majority of the twenty-three years I have been living with a chronic illness. These concepts, Reflection, Realization, and Perception gave me the ability to examine where I've been, what I've done, and the potential impact I could have on others.

Almost two decades later, I was sitting in a philosophy class and we were asked to reflect on, and write about a traumatic experience in our lives. It was then that I was able to begin to understand both the question I had pondered for so long and its answer. The following paragraph is a part of what I wrote:

"How different would I be today if October 9th, 1983 never happened. I can only wonder. There I was surrounded by smart people with dumb looks on their faces and not a single person in that room could answer the one question I had, why did this happen? Everyone in that room patted me on my back, oh how I hate to be patted on my back. They told me that everything would be ok. I thought to myself, if you can't answer my question then how do you know everything will be ok? I sat in that hospital bed and bravely smiled. If I would have known the obstacles that lay ahead I don't think I would I have been so brave. I felt my childhood get up and leave. I watched as it walked right out of that hospital room never to be seen again. I was ten years old and being asked to deal with what most adults would need a prescription for extra strength Vicodin and several years of intensive counseling to deal with. I was ten years old and being asked if I understood what four doctors with sixty years of combined experience could not even begin to explain. I was ten years old and trying to get the only question I had answered, why?"

Before I could begin my treatments I needed to have a dialysis access placed. With everything that had happened at Children's Hospital during my kidney biopsy the doctors decided that it would be best if they took me to the operating room to perform the procedure under general anesthesia. Before they could do that they needed to perform a test. The test I am speaking of was yet another in a mounting list of traumatic experiences that only perpetuated the fear and anger building inside of me.

My kidney function had finally come to a grinding halt and everything that I drank accumulated in my body. I was eventually admitted to the University Of Minnesota Hospital which at that time was known throughout the country for its Pediatric Nephrology program as a leader in the treatment of children with kidney disease. The University Of Minnesota was one of only a few hospitals that would provide dialysis treatments for children with ESRD (End Stage Renal Disease).

By the time October 9th, 1983 came around I had accumulated almost eighty pounds of excess fluid and was very close to dying. The fluid was being deposited throughout my vascular system but what worried my doctors the most was the fact that the fluid's concentration was around my heart and in my lungs. My heart was working overtime and I struggled to breathe. It was at this point that the pediatric nephrology team decided that I needed to begin dialysis. The problem was that I was very sick and they were not sure if the excess fluid in my body contained bacteria that could potentially lead to a fatal infection after surgery. So they ordered a tap to be performed and I was taken into a treatment room. I was so scared that I began to cry and scream as soon as I saw what I could only now describe as an instrument that looked like a tap that you would see on an old wooden barrel of beer. I fought, kicked, and screamed, and it took several people to hold me down as they inserted that sharp, long faucet right into my belly. The sample they obtained tested negative for bacteria and I was taken to the operating room for a Hickman catheter placement.

I awoke to a sharp pain in my right shoulder and a pressure bandage that was firmly taped to my chest. A plastic tube was bulging under the skin there as it snaked its way over the clavicle and deep into the main artery that would take it ever so close to my heart. As I ran my fingers up toward the right side of my neck I felt the stitches that protruded from the first of what would be many scars. I knew these scars were like tattoos, permanently providing a visual reference of a personal and traumatic experience.
Different smells and sensations have always had the ability to trigger my many fragmented memories of a childhood spent in a disease induced medical nightmare that would haunt and dictate many of the choices I made thru my mid-twenties.

One of those smells was Betadine. I remember it clearly because it always made me sick. The cold, wet, brown chemical had a distinctive odor that always made me shudder whenever the nurse would remove the old bandage covering the catheter and apply the medicated q-tip in a circular pattern at the point of intrusion. I even remember the instant salty taste in my mouth after the nurse injected my catheter with Heparin for the first time. To this day, every time I have to take Heparin I am immediately brought back to October 9th, 1983 and the first time I was wheeled into the dialysis center at the University Of Minnesota.

The hospital orderly who was in charge of patient transportation showed up at 7:45am to take me to the dialysis center for my first treatment. I had already been awake for hours just sitting in the dark alone with my thoughts. My mind was racing because I had no idea what to expect. Again I was overcome with fear. Yesterday the doctors and nurses tried to explain what the dialysis treatment process would involve, but the explanation seemed as cold as a metal instrument. There was no feeling, just the sterile description, almost automatic, like they had repeated those exact same lines to so many others before me. The hospital orderly entered my room with a wheel chair and said, "I am here to take you to see the great and mighty Wizard of Oz." I smiled and got out of bed. I could feel all of the extra water in my body as it sloshed back and forth like a full bucket of water being carried. I was fluid overloaded and walking around with an extra 80 lbs of water floating inside me. It felt like I was wearing deathly heavy, soaking wet clothing all the time, and it took everything I had to walk. I struggled to put one leg in front of the other. Both of my legs felt burdensome and I would describe my walking as similar to a king penguin; side to side, slowly.

The cold and sterile smell of the hospital pressed against my face as we raced from one hallway to another. The wheelchair ride into the unknown was the most fun I'd had in months. I wanted the orderly to go faster and faster. He was running because he had a list of patients he needed to transport to other clinics and was pressed for time. We turned the corner and suddenly stopped. I looked up at a pair of heavy wooden doors and watched as he pushed a button on the wall and they magically opened. Then he wheeled me into the dialysis unit and jokingly said, "Don't pay any attention to the man behind the green curtain." I barely caught what he'd said because I was preoccupied with the lions, and tigers, and bears (oh my) that lay ahead.

My eyes grew wide as I looked around and tried to absorb everything I was seeing. My wheelchair came to a stop and suddenly the hospital orderly was gone. In front of me was a giant lazy boy chair with a strange machine next to it. The machine had lots of tubing connected to it and was making quite a bit of noise. I heard a voice from a man who was standing in front of the machine with his back to me. "I'll be finished in a second." Then he promptly spun around and introduced himself as he helped me from my wheelchair into the lazy boy. "Hi, I'm Irv and I will be taking care of you today." Immediately I knew Irv was one of those guys that put you at ease. He had an air of reassurance about him.

I watched as he unclamped this and disconnected that. He seemed to know how to keep the strange machine I was gazing at quiet. Then Irv reached down and took the bandage off of my catheter and explained that he needed to clean everything before he could begin. Minutes later he connected a tube in the shape of a "y" and I watched as my blood left my body. I can still remember the chill that ran up my spine. As I watched, my teeth began to chatter and the sharp cold invaded my body. My hands turned deathly white and my fingers felt stiff. I started to feel like I couldn't breathe, and it seemed like I had a boulder on my chest.

I began to have a sharp pain in my spine that came and went every other second like a neon sign that flashed. I looked up at Irv and he could tell that something was wrong. He asked me how I felt and before I could finish describing what I was feeling he had almost rinsed all of my blood back into my body. After a few minutes the symptoms subsided and he began the dialysis process again. I sat and watched as the blood pump rotated for hours while a symphony of emotions played in my head. I just didn't have the ability to understand what was going on. I felt numb, fearful, and detached. The situation seemed surreal. I was unable to fully make any association and at that time I really didn't understand how dire the circumstances were. What I would come to understand, and the association I would eventually make, is that the process of kidney dialysis increased the physical and emotional deterioration I was experiencing. The disease process and the required treatments were a never-ending cycle that quickly stole what innocence I had left. I struggled to make sense out of everything and the one realization I had was that every minute I was getting worse. Everyday I was deteriorating. Imagine for a moment being ten years old and coming to that kind of a realization. Everyday I looked to my mother for protection as any frightened child would, and in her eyes I saw the same fear that I was feeling. It seemed that no matter what was attempted medically, the situation worsened. I was scared, and I did not want to die. I was a ten-year-old child being confronted with my own mortality; physically and emotionally unable to find any momentary comfort or protection from the monster that ravaged within.

This was the point in my life where it all began. This was ground zero; the point of origin that would define my physical and emotional state of existence and the dysfunction that I would carry with me for years to come. I was a ten-year-old child who was physically and emotionally broken.

That first dialysis treatment lasted several hours and they were able to successfully remove a total of six pounds of water from my body. During the process I experienced low blood pressure, severe muscle cramping, extreme chills, and vomiting. My head constantly pounded and I was having a hard time focusing my thoughts. I was so exhausted throughout the process and wanted to sleep but "the monster" made that all but impossible. It seemed liked days had passed before I was finally wheeled back to my hospital room and helped into bed. It felt good to crawl back in. I pulled the blanket close to my neck and asked for another. The heat from the two blankets started to bring feeling back into my feet and hands. The warmth brought a sense of peace that felt like a much-needed hug. The type of hug my mother would give me. I closed my eyes and embraced the darkness hoping to hide and escape from "the monster" for at least a few hours. Eventually I began to nod off but would awake to the violent throws and retching of my body as it seized and cramped. I reached for a basin and threw up repeatedly. The entire process lasted several minutes. Relief was momentarily brief and then the process would repeat itself. This continued for the next twelve hours.

That whole first experience left me physically drained and emotionally numb for days. It seemed that my body and the medical team with its procedures, drugs, surgeries, and treatments were in an epic battle. The body was doing what it was designed to do; trying to fight off this evil attack while the medical team, like Generals during the civil war, calculated stratagems and used everything they could to stave off the impending onslaught of the disease.

I could see the battle being waged everyday during rounds. There was the look of calculation and determination on each and every one of my doctor's faces. The group of them unwilling to concede. They were determined to hold the line at all costs. Steadfast and resolute in their ability to save my life.

In writing this chapter and reliving my past, I have come to realize that I never did officially thank those generals or the army of professionals who took care of me as an angry and fearful child. It is because of all of you that I grew, developed, and prospered. It is because of all of you that I survived the war.

To this day I still carry with me the physical and emotional scars from battles won and lost in a war that lasted for years. That war finally ended in a negotiated peace. One that allowed for growth and development and that over the years has fostered prosperity. You see, out of that growth and development came **Reflection, Realization,** and **Perception,** and with it my ability to realize that during the war I acted like a spy who was determined to create insurgency.

It was my fear and anger that cried for war. It was fear and anger about a disease that ravaged my body and stole my childhood that led me on a rampage of self-destruction. I was unable to see a future so I lived for the moment and tried to forget every hope and dream I ever had. It was just the three of us, fear, anger, and me working in unison to cultivate my defiant personality. That defiance lasted fifteen years and eventually led my battle worn emotions to the realization of peaceful co-existence based on a fundamental change in how I perceived the world around me.

"Realize that you are more than your diagnosis and your perception will begin to change. Realize that you have goals and dreams, ask questions, seek answers, and strive to achieve; your world will transform right before your eyes." Shad Ireland 07/04

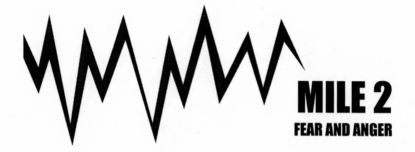

MILE 2
FEAR AND ANGER

Fear and anger are a lethal combination. Together they have the ability to trigger the fight or flight response and with the childhood I had prior to my illness I knew nothing of flight. I have always been a fighter. It is all that I know.

My biological father was an angry man. He beat my mother, my brother, and me whenever he became upset. I was five years old and vividly remember him standing over my mother after she fell in the kitchen from one of his punches. He screamed at her as he dumped flour and sugar on the floor and ran his feet through the white powder back and forth making it unusable. He did it because he knew my mother loved to bake. Baking was something that she did as a child with her mother and it made her happy. As far as he was concerned happiness was not allowed. After his tirade, he stormed off to the bedroom and slammed the door. I watched as my mother pulled herself off of the floor and brushed the white dusting from her clothes. She said she was ok and that everything would be all right. Soon my fear for my mother turned into anger. Here I was, five years old and plotting a hate crime. The emotions I felt boiled throughout my body as I glared at the closed bedroom door. My mother told me to go and play in my room so I went and colored. A couple of hours later he was yelling again and this time it was our turn to feel his anger.

I watched as he had my brother bend over the love seat and pull his pants down. I heard the crack of the belt against my brother's skin and he began to cry. Crack! Crack! Crack! With each one I shook with terror. I am not sure how many times he hit my brother but after he went running by into our bedroom I knew it was my turn.

He yelled for me to get into the living room. I cautiously approached with tears in my eyes. "What did I do wrong? Please don't hit me daddy," I pleaded, but my cries and pleas fell on deaf ears. He was so consumed with pain and anger that he wanted us to hurt too. He told me to pull down my pants and I said no. This only enraged him. He grabbed me by my arm and ripped my pants down. He hit me so hard with that belt, and so many times that the sting lasted for hours. When he finished I pulled up my pants and turned to look at him. I had the Devil in my eyes. I was going to kill him. I was five years old and so filled with hate. I have never experienced anger like that since. We locked eyes and for a second I think he knew. I told him to wait till he went to sleep.

The next thing I knew he was choking me and slamming my body against the wall. He had one hand around my throat and used the other to hold my mother at bay. I remember her grabbing him screaming, "DICK YOU ARE GOING TO KILL HIM." He finally dropped me on the floor and stormed out of the apartment. My mother picked me up and held me in her arms. We were both crying. He never came home that night.

The next time I saw him was the following morning at the breakfast table. He never even acknowledged my presence. He just ate his cereal and stared off into the distance content to ignore us all.

Even though both of my parents were college educated and worked professionally as Registered Nurses our family struggled financially. My biological father worked overnights and my mother worked first or second shift. Sometimes she worked double shifts for extra money. They only saw each other on weekends which I believe only contributed to the mounting stress in our home. I would learn many years later that during this time he turned to selling drugs for extra money and rather quickly became an addict.

It began almost immediately after my mother left for work. She was scheduled to work a twelve-hour shift that Saturday and would arrive home to find her life turned upside down. My biological father seemed to run around the house franticly. I followed him into the kitchen and watched as he emptied the ice cube trays into the sink, put the salt and peppershakers into a plastic bag, and packed everything he could put his hands on into a box. He turned and looked at me with a scowl on his face, "What do you want?" he said. "What are you doing? Why are you packing? Are we moving?" I asked. "No, go sit on the couch and watch TV with your brother" he yelled. I walked over to the couch and watched as he set the box by the front door. I noticed that he kept looking at his watch. He walked back into their bedroom and I cautiously followed. I peeked around the bedroom door and watched as he opened my mother's jewelry box and shoved everything into his pockets. I always loved the sweet sounds it made when you opened it. There were times when I would sneak into my parent's bedroom and lift the top of that jewelry box open so I could hear the music. It always made me think of my mother.

I stood in the moment, and as the music played I forgot where I was. My biological father's head snapped sideways and our eyes

24

locked. For a moment he pondered whether or not I saw what he did. I stood there unable to move, frozen stiff for fear of another beating. I think he realized that I knew his treacherous plot and like the snake he was he struck viciously fast. The sensation of pain from the bite of his angry venom would last for several days. With one hand he grabbed my arm and dragged me down the hall while repeatedly beating me on my backside with the other. He opened the door to the bedroom I shared with my brother and threw me toward the bunk bed. I hit my shin on the rail and collapsed on the lower bunk. The pain was instant. I thought that my leg had shattered. The swelling was immediate and the grapefruit sized black and blue mark looked like I had and additional kneecap. He raised his hand into a fist and ran toward the bed. Then he stood over me and paused.

I could see his fangs as he considered another strike. He told me that if I kept crying he would really give me something to cry about. So I wiped my tears and stifled the crying best I could. "That's better," he said as he turned, walked out, and calmly shut the door. That was the last time I remember seeing him until I was quite a bit older.

I don't know how many hours had passed before I got up the courage to leave my bedroom. I eventually ventured out and joined my brother on the couch where he was watching TV. I sat there for hours and stared out of the sliding glass door as the last bit of daylight I would see for years turned into blackness. It was on that Saturday that the consuming fire of anger and blackness totally invaded my soul. It was my biological father's self-hatred, anger, and blackness that infected my innocence.

The sound of a key being put into the lock of the apartment door struck fear and apprehension throughout my body. Was it HIM coming home? What would he do if he found me out of my bedroom and on the couch watching TV? I limped as fast as I could back to the bedroom but the apartment door swung open and the external hallway light illuminated my tiny frame. There I was standing in front of my bedroom door caught in the act. My mind raced as the possible excuses started to pour out. I was stopped mid-sentence as tears of joy began to roll down my cheeks. My mother was home and I limped over to her and hugged her as tight as I could. "Where is your brother? Why are all of the lights turned out? Where is your father? Why are you not in your Pajama's? Have you eaten dinner yet?" The answers to those questions would eventually lead her to our biological father's treacherous desertion. A desertion that was designed to break her both emotionally and physically, but a desertion that would backfire. His treachery only elevated our mother. Her purity of character and love for her children gave her the strength to persevere. It would be that love for us that carried her through the long, difficult, and challenging years that would follow.

Upon reflecting back to this time in my life I am personally confronted with the memories of my actions and behavior. The anger and blackness, like a cancer, rapidly spread throughout my body and like a miniature version of my biological father I became violent. These random and steady outbursts were a direct result of the long-term exposure and consequential infection of a man who was so completely filled with self-hatred, anger, and blackness. To this day, I have a hard time referring to him as a man because I feel that even this term is not deserved. Instead I refer to him as my biological father whenever he is mentioned. He simply does not deserve the respect that using his first name would provide. Later in life I would be given what he would call an explanation. But what I thought then, and still continue to consider, is that moreover, his explanation was simply an excuse to justify his actions and ultimately that treacherous desertion of so many years before.

After my mother's return that night, several days would pass that now are just blurry and faded memories. What I do remember next is an event that would eventually change my **Perception**. Although it took until my early twenties, the memory of this event triggered the initial glimpse into my ability to **Reflect**, **Realize**, and **Perceive**. It was this event that would crack the window and begin to allow daylight to filter out the blackness that filled my mind, body, and soul. You see for many years I thought my mother did not love me. That it was somehow my fault that my biological father beat us and eventually left. It was **Reflection** that brought about **Realization** and this **Realization** changed how I perceived my mother for the rest of her life.

It was dinnertime and I was so hungry. We were going to have one of my favorite meals; a chicken potpie. I looked at my brother who sat next to me on the couch with his TV tray in front of him and a steamy potpie fresh from the oven. It made my mouth water. My TV tray was empty but I knew my mother was going to bring me one too. She came into the living room carrying only one plate. She set the plate on my TV tray and proceeded to sit down on the love seat. I dug right in and took a huge bite burning the roof of my mouth. I remember sucking in as much air as I could to cool everything because I was too hungry to spit it out and wait for it to cool on its own. I looked at my mother who barely squeezed out a smile. After about a minute I was able to swallow the hot, flaky and tasty bite I had in my mouth. I went to take another bite and realized that she was missing her plate. "Where is your potpie?" I asked. She again smiled and told me that she was not hungry. I hadn't seen her eat anything that night or the day before. Our fridge and cupboards were almost bare and I was beginning to realize my mother hadn't any money.

It was the memory of this event that triggered the initial glimpse into my ability to **Reflect**, **Realize**, and **Perceive**. It allowed me to begin to understand and Realize the years of sacrifices she made for the love of her children, and how much she really loved me.

During my childhood I treated her like my biological father had, I kicked and hit, yelled and screamed, but she never abandoned me. It got to a point where she was unable to deal with my violent outbursts. Years later, she shared with me the day that brought her to the decision that in her words, broke her heart.

I used to walk to school because we lived in a part of town that did not have bussing. I enjoyed those long walks because I got a chance to play with my imaginary friends. Army was my favorite game. We were the Americans and the Germans for some reason all looked like my biological father. We killed a lot of Germans on those long walks but there would always be more of them waiting for us after school. It was during recess that it happened. A couple of second graders were playing with a ball so I walked over and asked if I could play too. They both laughed at me and got the other children to join in. I became enraged. The anger and blackness clouded my vision. I did not see two-second graders. I saw what looked like my biological father.

I turned around and walked away but the anger and blackness kept building inside of me. I walked over to a pole and noticed a bike chain lying on the ground. I picked it up and in a split second I was running at both of those second graders. I let the first one have it right across the face and turned to catch the second one as he started to run. I caught him on the back of the head and watched as he dropped to the ground. I shouted a few profanities and told them to stop crying or I would give them something to cry about. The teachers on the playground were horrified. I put the chain down and calmly walked away. I was immediately taken to the principal's office and my mother was called to school. The first question asked of my mother was if everything was ok at home. The principal told her she'd never seen that kind of rage in a child and asked if I had been abused. My mother denied any abuse and tried to talk the principal out of expelling me from school. Instead she gave my mother the number for a counseling service and told her I was not allowed anywhere near the school property.

The ride home was filled with my mother yelling at me. She never hit my brother or me. Instead she just yelled and this time it was "What am I going to do with you? I can't take you to work with me" and then she began to cry.

With everything that had happened over the years and as my daily violent outbursts became more and more uncontrollable my mother was pushed to her breaking point. Several years ago, my mother and I talked about this period of our lives. She shared with me the story of how she was faced with two options and how the anger and blackness almost infected her. She told me about the night she almost killed me.

I was curled up in her lap sound asleep. It was the only time the house was peaceful. She told me how she loved the peace and quiet. That during those times she finally got her chance, to relax. How she wanted it to stay that way. She would watch me sleep and run her fingers through my hair. Then she realized how easy it would be to smother me. She felt the anger and blackness from the years of abuse and when I became uncontrollable it reminded her of my biological father. Again she thought of how easy it would be to smother me, in essence smothering her ex-husband. She told me how these thoughts scared her and how she began to cry. She felt like she was a bad mother and had somehow failed me. It was at that moment she knew she had to get help. She called the number that the principal gave her and talked with a crisis counselor. They told her about an organization called the Wilder Foundation and that they could help both of us. That phone call she made and her decision to get help that night saved my life. The following day she spoke with a few professionals at Wilder and the consensus was that I immediately needed residential treatment and intensive one-on-one counseling. The trick was getting me to the facility.

The decision she made to place me at Wilder only perpetuated the anger and blackness that pulsed through my veins. I felt abandoned, first by my biological father, and now her. For years I made her pay for those feelings of abandonment. Yet for all the pain I gave she returned it with unconditional love. Years later when I asked her why she never gave up on me she said she could never abandon me because I was her little boy.

My mother would take me home on weekend visits and when Sunday came it was time to take me back. I would kick and scream and beg and plead but she did what she had too. She took me back and before she left she would promise to come get me next weekend and she would. Almost every weekend she brought me home. She was a mother who worked two jobs and went to night school. She was a mother who loved her two children even though one of those children told her he never loved her.

It was in 1992 when I finally began to understand and **Realize** what an amazing woman she always was. You see for years my mother gave better than she ever got from me and even though I apologized, and even though I knew she loved me and understood why I acted the way I did, I will carry with me to my grave the personal remorse for the pain I caused her during my childhood.

I should have realized earlier the woman she was and everything she had gone through for the love of her children. I was her son and she deserved better from me.

I have always loved to travel. As a child U-hauls fascinated me. I was born in the great state of retirement and I remember moving back and forth from Arizona to Minnesota several times in a U-haul. I would get excited every time my parents told me to pack my suitcase. I had a split pea green Samsonite and all of my clothes when neatly folded would fit in the bottom compartment. So one day when my mother called me in from playing outside and told me to pack all of my clothes in my suitcase I was filled with excitement. I could not stop asking questions. "Where are we going?" "Where is the U-haul?" As I approached the car I noticed that neither my brothers nor mothers suitcases were in or near it. I suspiciously asked, "Where are your suitcases?" My mother quickly responded "In the trunk." I asked if I could put my suitcase in the trunk with theirs but I was told it was full and I would have to keep mine in the back seat with me. I had an uneasy feeling in my gut that something was not right. My brother and mother seemed nervous.

We drove for twenty minutes and eventually stopped outside of this large two story brown brick building. I knew something was wrong. My mother told my brother to wait in the car and told me to come with her. I looked at her suspiciously and did as I was told. She told me we were here to see one of her friends and that it would only take a minute. That was a lie. I remember walking in first and the heavy metal door slammed behind me. I quickly turned around and looked out of the window as my mother's eyes filled with tears and she turned and walked away. I screamed and yelled for her, "WAIT COME BACK" but she could not hear me through the heavy metal door. I was screaming and crying trying to open it. Why would she do this to me? I didn't understand what was going on. Then I felt a hand on my shoulder as I was spun around. In front of me stood three people I had never met before in my life and they told me that this was going to be my new home. The tears dried up and the anger and blackness took over. One of these strangers went to grab my shoulder and walk me away from the door. As soon as I felt the hand on my shoulder I let her have it. I wanted to go home. I tried to run but the other one grabbed me. I saw a fire extinguisher on the wall and grabbed for it. It came off of the wall with ease so I pointed it at them and squeezed the handle. They all got a face full of white powder. I was frantic.

I didn't know where I was, and I had no idea where to run. So I started to run down some stairs but found the door locked. I was trapped. I kicked and screamed and fought, but I was no match for three adults. It took all three of them though to hold me down. They physically restrained me for an hour and a half until I had nothing left. I was eventually let up off the ground and taken to the bathroom to clean up, then given dinner and a tour of my new prison. After that I was led to the shower and given a towel and my pajamas. I had my own room which consisted of a desk, a dresser, a chair, a small window and a twin mattress that had my split pea green Samsonite on it. I was then told I had fifteen minutes to unpack my clothes and put them in my dresser before I had to go to sleep. Fifteen minutes later the counselor came back and turned my light out and shut the door.

The room felt spooky and I missed having my brother in the bed above me. I was angry with my mother and never wanted to see her again. I was afraid of the shadows on the wall because they all reminded me of my biological father. I thought they we coming to get me. It was that night that I became afraid of the dark. It's funny, I am thirty-two years old and to this day I still sleep with a light on.

The next morning I awoke to the smell of cinnamon french toast. I was startled when I awoke because I did not know where I was. Slowly the memories from yesterday came back to me as I wiped the sleep from my eyes. I got out of bed and proceeded to get dressed. I walked out into the hallway and followed all of the other kids downstairs. We had to line up in a single file line in front of the kitchen and stand there quietly. We were each called into the dining room by our first name. We waited until everyone was seated and then we were instructed to take two french toast and pass the plate. Next the sausage, take one sausage link and pass the plate we were told. After everyone was served we were allowed to eat. After breakfast we all helped clear the table and I was given the privilege of vacuuming the dining room; my first chore. After clean up duty I was given another tour and introduced to the staff that worked the morning shift. They had a total of three shifts; morning, evening, and overnight. I had the rules explained to me and then I was let outside to play with the other children. I couldn't believe it. They were letting me outside. Now was my chance. I stood around and kicked a couple of rocks. I looked to my left, no staff, then to my right, no staff. I watched as the other kids played with a kick ball and wondered why none of them were running as fast as they could from this place. I was six years old and planning my great escape.

I ran away that day, and every day I got the chance to run away, I did it again. I liked the freedom, and no matter how long they made me stand in the corner, every chance I got I ran. Eventually I would find the freedom I craved in the very thing that I thought would get me out of that place but never did.

I was first introduced to the sport of running at the age of eight. At one of the counselors' meetings they'd had a discussion about me. Since I used to like to run away, they decided that maybe by training to be a runner I could learn some discipline. Frank, one of the counselors, was into running and volunteered to teach me the sport. I remember I was never really given an option but rather, told that I could run everyday with Frank or stand in the corner for an hour. I chose to run. So everyday we would run for an hour. We would talk while we ran and I quickly developed a deep respect for Frank. I remember the day he told me he was leaving. I felt abandoned again, but Mike Garr, another counselor, took over where Frank had left off and we became fast friends too. Everyone could see what a positive impact the daily training and one-on-one interaction had on me and so it was considered part of my treatment plan. I don't know if they ever knew but running helped to ease the emotional pain that I carried with me and gave me the freedom I craved. When I was outside running I didn't have to think about anything else. I just focused on my breathing and everything else seemed to fade away. I used that same technique when I initially began training to become the first dialysis patient to ever compete in and complete an Ironman. The physical and emotional pain from years of dealing with a chronic illness seemed to fade away whenever I trained. As I became stronger my confidence grew just like when I was an eight-year-old child. I remember the day Mike suggested I should compete in a race. I became excited; my very first race. The Jewish Community Center where Mike had a membership was having a fun run and he signed me up. It was a two-mile race and I had dreams of winning.

I finished the race and took 4th place overall with a time of 16:53. For the first time in my life I felt like I had accomplished something positive. My mother, brother, and Mike were all there cheering for me as I crossed my first finish line. I looked up to Mike like a father figure. At night I used to ask God why I couldn't have a father like Mike.

I lived at Wilder for a total of three years. Over those years I received an education, counseling, and love from all of the staff members. One of those staff members was Sheryl Anderson. She really cared about me, and all of the children she worked with. She spent hours on the phone with my mother and they developed a friendship, which lasted for twenty-six years. Two other counselors besides Sheryl made a huge impression on me during those three years and I can't remember the last time I spoke to either of them. I heard from Sheryl that Dave Cook is now a practicing psychologist, and I found out that Mike Garr left Wilder and decided to go to medical school.

It's funny how small the world really is sometimes. At the age of twenty-one I would find myself laying in a coma fighting for my life and whom do you think my mother would run into in an elevator at the University Of Minnesota hospital? None other than Dr. Michael Garr, now a Cardiologist there, but that story I will save for a later chapter.

By the time I left Wilder I was very good at pretending to be a happy, articulate, outgoing, and social child, but I used that to hide the pain that I felt deep inside. When I look at pictures of myself during those years I see the duality. If you looked deep enough into my eyes they would tell you the entire story. Deep down I was hurting, and ruled by the dark and grey storm clouds that had hovered over me for so many years. The anger from an abusive childhood continued to loom on the horizon and my diagnosis at the age of ten would be the catalyst that brought the storm crashing to shore. I wrote a poem once about the eyes being the windows to the soul. Maybe that is why to this day children always make me smile. In their eyes I can see the wonder and amazement they feel. It is that wonder and amazement that reminds me of a childhood I dreamed of nightly; one filled with exuberant screams and laughter. A childhood that was not my own.

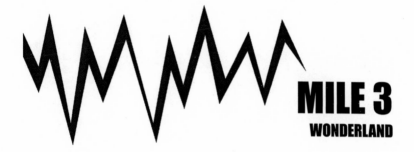

MILE 3
WONDERLAND

By the age of sixteen I had gone through numerous surgeries, and was struggling to find the emotional capacity to deal with my daily routine. The emotional and physical drain I experienced from having this illness and the required treatments to stay alive, felt unbearable most of the time. I have to admit that during those dark years of my life I often thought about suicide. I spent countless hours in the bathroom vomiting. My head was constantly pounding from having high blood pressure, and the medication I took to control it would cause severe cases of dizziness and fainting spells due to the extreme fluctuations in my blood pressure throughout the day. What little energy I did have was consumed during the six-hour dialysis process every Monday, Wednesday, and Friday. I was consistently exhausted. I looked in the mirror and was terrified at what I saw. My skin was ghostly white; my eyes sunken in, and I could see every bone in my rib cage. It was impossible for me to gain any weight and similar to a patient undergoing chemotherapy, everything I ate had a metallic taste to it. I was barely alive.

I was embarrassed by my physical appearance and my inability to do the simple things other kids my age could do. School was a nightmare. My illness kept me from completing a lot of my homework. The teachers I had were sympathetic so they required little effort from me. If I attended class I got a passing grade. I dreamed of playing sports in high school but always sat and watched the other children during physical education. I was different and I hated that this was my reality. I was at an age when I was starting to notice girls but yet they were not noticing me. I looked at other guys my age who were developing and turning into men while I remained five feet tall and 90 lbs.

As time passed, that isolation I felt from everyone continued to grow and as it did it only fed the anger, frustration, and self-hatred I had. I wanted others to feel the pain and hopelessness that pulsed through my veins. Every Monday, Wednesday, and Friday I exploded. The doctors and nurses received the full brunt of my rage. I was isolated and desperate. I looked at the other children who were so sick and it seemed to me that they were resolved to accept this as their fate. I could not and would not. I remember the madness that raced through my mind. Somehow I came to believe that the doctors and nurses were to blame for my deterioration. That somehow they were directly contributing to the annihilation of my existence. As I progressively got worse and the side effects from receiving dialysis treatments increased, my anger, frustration, depression, and isolation grew. Emotionally and physically I was a wreck. I felt tormented and wanted desperately for it all to end. While others dreamed of transplantation and waited for the phone call that would change their lives, I was told that I was not transplantable. Due to the numerous amounts of blood transfusions I had received during the first few years of dialysis treatments my body had built up an immune response and my antibody level reached 100%. This meant that I had no hope of getting a transplant. I wanted to die. I truly felt that no one understood the desperation, anger, fear and hopelessness that was, my life. That hopelessness I was feeling however was about to change, briefly anyway.

Hope is a very powerful thing, because it has the ability to instantly change an individual's perception and dramatically impact his/her life. Let me start by telling you that it had been years since I had urinated. In fact, it had been so long that I had forgotten what it felt like to pee. One day I had the urge. It came about rather suddenly so I ran to the bathroom and to my surprise urine started coming out like water out of a hose. These urges became more frequent and it was not long before my dialysis treatments were cut back to two times a week.

My kidneys were beginning to function again and I was hopeful that maybe I would no longer need dialysis. Then, came my devastation two months later when the well dried up and I needed to go back on dialysis three times a week. I asked my doctors why but no one really had an answer. All they could say was that my kidneys began to function again. This brief reprieve gave me a false sense of hope, so the return to my former routine only accelerated my downward spiral. I went back to feeling hopeless and became even angrier than before. I could not see my life improving at all. I was sixteen years old and I had reached the end of my rope. It was then that I first tried to commit suicide.

I came home from dialysis on a Friday night and went straight to my room. As usual I felt barely alive and tonight was the night I had decided to end it all. I wanted to go to sleep and never wake up. So I thought to myself, what would be the easiest way to do this? I decided I was going to OD.

I was on three different medications for blood pressure and figured that if I took a handful of pills and went to bed that it would all be over. I headed to the kitchen and poured myself a tall glass of cold water, grabbed one of the bottles of blood pressure medication, and walked back into my room, quietly shutting the door. I stayed there for over an hour just sitting on the edge of my bed contemplating the decision I was about to make. I thought about how peaceful it would be to just go to sleep and never wake up. So I poured the pills into my hand, then popped them into my mouth, and swallowed them all. I could feel the entire glass of water glide down my throat, and then I simply waited to fall asleep. To my utter shock and disappointment, I awoke the next morning and began to cry. I was sure that I had taken more than enough pills to do the job. I guess I came at least somewhat close because as soon as I stood up, I collapsed.

The room was spinning and my head hurt. I lay on the floor and the tears ran down my face. I spent twelve hours lying there unable to really move. By early evening I was able to pick myself up and crawl back into bed.

My inability to take my own life left me feeling even more depressed. I was filled with hopelessness and despair. An overwhelming sense of emptiness set in as I spent the next few weeks walking through my life in a fog. I was in a lot of physical and emotional pain, desperate to escape yet chained to my situation.

The long-term exposure I had to these powerful emotions of anger, fear, loss of self-autonomy and control had an adverse effect and negative influence on my development and outlook on life. In order to survive, I had to adapt. It was either that or surrender and die. I turned off my feelings and became numb to the world. As a result, I developed an attitude and started not caring and being very cold to everyone I came in contact with. I was like fire and Ice. When I became angry I exploded and when people tried to reach out to me I froze them out. I just didn't care, and as hard as I tried, I could not escape from what I felt inside. I was emotionally being torn apart.

By this time I had been receiving kidney dialysis treatments for over six years and it was shortly after my first suicide attempt, sometime around the middle of the sixth year that my body began to adapt and stabilize. Those six and a half years seemed like an eternity, but eventually I settled into the routine that was my life. Not only had I become very good at being cold and sterile toward everyone around me, I replicated that feeling toward the effects of dialysis. I adapted and incorporated the medical misery into my daily routine with a little help from some recreational acquaintances. Eventually, these acquaintances would become good friends.

It was only a matter of time before I would formally be introduced to the term "recreational use". I felt like I needed to medicate the pain because my inability to cope with my life was pushing me over the edge. I was unable to find an outlet for the anger, fear, and frustration I felt, so this became the one way I could deal.

I was unable to communicate through the darkness that surrounded me. These emotions came with the diagnosis and grew stronger as the disease process progressed.

Partying and recreational use went hand in hand and I spent over nine years immersed in that life. The seduction began the very first time I walked into *After the Gold Rush*. *"The Rush"* as it was called, would fill to capacity at least two nights a week. On Sunday nights they had 16 plus events (you had to be at least 16 years old to enter) and on Thursday nights they had 18 plus events (you had to be at least 18 years old to enter). Since I quickly developed a reputation, an ID was not required of me. *"The Rush"* had an amazing light show and for a five-dollar cover charge I was able to visit Wonderland for a few hours. Like Alice, I too would fall down the rabbit hole and find myself at the Mad Hatter's party with an interesting group of characters. At first I watched cautiously, but eventually I too became one of those interesting characters and found myself with a teacup in hand.

It started, as only two nights a week. From 9 pm until 1 am I began to meet people and make friends, I was introduced to the sub culture of clubbing. Like my illness, this lifestyle became all encompassing. I not only visited Wonderland I moved into the neighborhood and eventually found myself at after parties that lasted until 6 am the following morning. I would usually wake up in people's homes that I didn't personally know, yet that never seemed to matter.

It was only a matter of time before I sat at the head of the table and had my turn as the Mad Hatter. This is the cycle of life in Wonderland. Everyone eventually succumbs to the madness. I began to supplement my daily prescriptions with a steady infusion of alcohol and narcotics. This infusion made Wonderland and all the characters and the adventures we shared together much more enjoyable. I had a fatalistic view and was living a very fast life that

40

was self centered, irresponsible, and reckless.

Reflection allows individuals to achieve a semblance of understanding toward some of the things in their lives. It is this understanding that gave me the insight into how I came to the choices I made, how my perception affected my decision making process, and why some of those choices didn't seem at the time, like the wrong ones to make.

I met my best friend Troy sixteen years ago after one of the many parties I attended, and the adventures we've shared, have kept me laughing through it all. It's funny, when I look back at this period in my life and at the choices I've made, I can honestly say that if given the opportunity I wouldn't change a thing.

When I first met Troy I liked him immediately. He had a personality that was larger than life and he was brash and loud like me. I had just walked into my apartment when the phone rang. I looked at the clock and it was 1:15 am. I assumed it was Joy (the girl I was dating at the time), so I thought about not answering the phone. I had a good buzz going and she was definitely a buzz kill. Joy had nothing really going for her except looks and that was why I was with her. She wanted a relationship, wanted to share emotions, talk on the phone for hours, and I was too preoccupied with myself. I said the things she wanted to hear to keep her around but I really didn't care for her. She was making more and more demands on my time and I'd had about all I could take. I answered the phone expecting to hear her voice. I was going to tell her to lose my number but to my surprise it was Jenny.

Jenny was a party girl. I don't remember where I met her but she was the type of girl that was fun to hang out with. Jenny told me that she and a girlfriend were going to Perkins (a restaurant everyone hung out at after partying) and wanted to know if I wanted to go with. I tried to turn down the offer but she would not take no for an answer. She said they would be at my place in just a few minutes so I went outside and waited for them to arrive. The streetlights illuminated the front of my apartment building and the air was crisp. I took a deep breath and listened as that air filled my lungs. It was even more still and eerily quiet than a cemetery. I loved the night though. I lived downtown for the action but appreciated times like this.

About five minutes later they pulled up and I got into the back seat.

We headed to the south side of town and within minutes we pulled up in front of a nice white house. Jenny killed the headlights and turned off the car. I asked her what she was doing and she said that we were picking up her friend Troy. A minute later a silhouette emerged from the darkness. He staggered and stumbled a bit as he approached the car. The back door opened and in jumped the guy who I had no clue would turn out to be one of my best friends in life. Jenny made the introduction and he said to me, "My name is Troy but my friends call me T-Money." I shook his hand as Jenny pulled off. He was drunk and quite loud but we hit it off right away, talking for a minute only to discover that we had quite a few mutual friends. We spent a few hours at Perkins laughing and having a good time and before long it was time to finally call it a night.

We arrived back at my apartment and I stumbled out of Jenny's car. It was 5:23am, another long night. I walked up the stairs and down the hallway to my door. I could smell my neighbor's coffee brewing. It was Thursday morning and while others were getting up to start their day and head to work I was still drunk and heading to bed.

Suddenly, I awoke to a loud buzzing sound. I lifted my head off the pillow and glanced over at the clock. 3:34 pm. I got up and walked over to the intercom and pushed the speaker button. "Who is it?" I said. "Its Troy bro let me in."

I pushed the speaker button again and said "Who?" And the voice over the intercom said "It's Troy from last night, Perkins, buzz me in bro." I had to stop and think for a minute, and then I remembered who he was so still half dazed and asleep, I buzzed him in.

A minute later my apartment door opened and in walked Troy. He asked me what I was doing and so I told him I had just woken up. He laughed and asked me if I knew what time it was, adding that the bar he worked at opened at 4pm and he was buying breakfast. That was all I needed to hear. I grabbed a sweatshirt, put on my shoes, and out the door we went.

I loved living downtown because everything was within walking distance. I didn't have a car at that time and I hated taking the bus. It only took us about ten minutes to walk to where we were going and since I was quite hungry, I was looking forward to eating.

We arrived at *"Juke Box Saturday Night"* and walked in. We sat at the bar, but when I asked the bartender for a menu, he looked at me like a deer caught in headlights. Troy laughed and ordered "the special." I looked at Troy and asked him what the special was. Clearly I should have seen what was coming next. "Two for ones!" he cried, as if I should have known! The bartender then asked Troy if he wanted the usual and he nodded. While we waited for the drinks, Troy grabbed two cigarettes out of his pack and gave me one. I asked him for his lighter and lit the cigarette. Seconds later the bartender brought over four *"Colorado Bulldogs"* and said the first round was on him. Troy looked at me and plainly stated what I'm certain he felt was already obvious. "This is the breakfast of champions" and we both laughed. By 4:45 pm, we were both drunk again. (although I don't think I was totally sober from the previous night yet) Between the two of us we drank ten of those *"Colorado Bulldogs"* and polished off an entire pack of cigarettes. I could barely walk. I don't remember how I got home but what brought me back to reality was the all too familiar spray from the toilet hitting my face.

Between the night before and that day, I'd had far too much to drink and clearly, I was paying for it now. That spray from the toilet water though, was something I was quite used to. Since I had spent the last six years hovering over toilets throwing up after dialysis, it didn't bother me. It was all part of the routine.

I awoke later to find myself still slumped over the toilet and a little confused. It took me a minute to realize where I was. I had vomit on my sweatshirt and my body hurt from sleeping slumped over the toilet. The smell was awful so I quickly undressed and jumped into the shower. It felt really good and after about a half hour I felt like a new man. As per usual I had no concept of time. All I knew was that I was awake and ready to begin my day. Then I walked out into the living room and looked outside the window to see that it was pitch black. I glanced at the clock. 2:30 am. So I sat down on the couch and picked up the cordless phone. There was always an after party; I just needed to find a ride. In looking back at this chapter, I can say there are things I wouldn't change but I'm also not proud of many of the things I've done, and it's not my intention to glorify this period of my life. I do believe though, that by sharing these experiences and the emotions that brought me to the decisions I made during that time, others can, and will relate because universally we all share similar emotions.

I struggled for quite awhile with the idea of full disclosure. I was not sure if I wanted to fully share with everyone this time in my life. I considered toning it down but didn't want to paint a reality that was different than the reality I truly lived. Even though I struggled with that choice, I know I came to the right conclusion. By honestly sharing these choices and experiences, other dialysis patients will see where I have been, and how I have been able to embrace acceptance, which resulted in a positive change in my life.

When I examine my intentions and look at the goals I have set for this book, the answer seems rather simple. I know that by sharing everything, as painful as it may personally be at times, I give myself the greatest opportunity to reach others and to allow every reader the ability to find a connection. We all share similar emotions that I alluded to earlier, and find those connections with others through similar experiences. These things are the seeds that allow the individual to start examining the possibility of change taking place in his/her life. That growth process consists of **Reflection**, **Realization** and **Perception**. When these are combined with individual inspiration anything can be accomplished. All you have to do is look at me, to see that it's true.

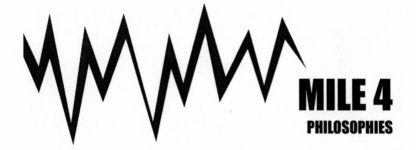

MILE 4
PHILOSOPHIES

The psychological-social impact this disease has on those who are diagnosed can be devastating. I couldn't understand the process, (the how or why) so I didn't expect to find understanding from others. The pain I felt was a very private and personal experience, and the lack of understanding only fuelled the anger that burned inside. Although I didn't understand the how or why, I rather quickly understood the loss of self-autonomy and control that this disease imposed. The scheduling and time commitments, fluid restriction, extreme dietary changes, copious amounts of medications, and hours of illness that followed each and every dialysis treatment resulted in causational behaviour. This loss of self-control, emotional isolation, and decrease in quality of life directly correlates to the primary issue of compliance and adherence that affects the majority of the dialysis population. If we can individually understand the process, we can then begin to transcend its causational effects.

I struggled with this for years before I reached a level of understanding that allowed me to transcend the issues and successfully develop a personal program defining the three life stages of a chronic illness; **Deal, Accept, Live**.

Deal, Accept, Live is a personal process that I developed after becoming the first dialysis patient to complete an Ironman triathlon. After the race in Lake Placid in July of 2004, I received thousands of emails from doctors, patients, and clinicians asking for my formula for success. **Deal, Accept, Live** combined with **Individual Inspiration** is that formula. This three-stage life changing process grew out of my initial introduction to the concepts of **Reflection**, **Realization**, and **Perception**. I was introduced to these concepts in a college philosophy class and will share that eye opening experience with you in a later chapter

Deal, Accept, Live is a seamless transitional process. When implemented with **Individual Inspiration** it will directly curb the causational behaviour that is a direct result of the emotional stress that this illness and the medical interventions required to maintain life impose. This process is a personal journey that will improve the quality of life not only for dialysis patients, but anyone diagnosed with a chronic illness. **Deal, Accept, Live** combined with **Individual Inspiration** simply defined, creates functional living out of the dysfunctional, destructive, emotionally and physically deteriorating progression of any chronic illness. This process consists of a dual approach implemented simultaneously,

47

which will successfully address both the emotional and physical needs of the individual diagnosed. In the following paragraphs I will delve into the specifics, providing you with the how and why, giving you a road map to take with you on your journey as you implement all that I've talked about.

Deal, Accept, Live

To "Deal" is the first step toward gaining back control over your life. The initial and hardest of the process begins by first being able to acknowledge the specific emotions. (Fear, anger, loss of self control, sense of unfairness, and the why me questioning) Start by thinking about your entire dialysis experience, from initial diagnosis to where you currently find yourself. What then works best is to pick up a pen and a piece of paper. Start writing down the emotions you associate with that experience. Take as much time as you need. And if you need to put it down and come back to it, do that. It took me several attempts before I felt that I had a complete list.

The next step in dealing with your reality is to ask questions and seek answers. The process I referred to earlier in the book, the "how and why", requires you to ask yourself the hard questions. Things like "How did I get to this point in my life?" "Why do I have these emotions and feelings?" For those and all questions, there will be answers, and they are the first of many obstacles you will face along your journey.

As frustrating and angry as you may feel about being sick, there is hope. Both your physical and emotional state can and will change. You need to always be cognoscente of that. I truly believe this because I've been there and have seen myself change the same way.

One of the many universal emotions we all share is hope. As patients, we hope that our situation will improve, but unfortunately this illness has the ability to create hopelessness. That hopelessness has such a powerful effect because it is reinforced by the physical deterioration we experience on a daily basis. For a dialysis patient, sometimes hope is hard to hold on to when we are faced with the daily struggles this illness imposes. It's easy to feel that all is lost and nothing can be done, and hard to maintain faith that life can be "normal" again. So to give up is easy, to want to live and to fight for it is the challenge we face.

Success is initially achieved when we are able to reconnect with hope. To have it, means the ability to believe that our situation can improve, and this rediscovery allows us to begin to take back control of our lives. It opens our eyes to the world around us and gives us the ability to initially perceive our situation as improving. Hope equals the ability to deal with any situation we find ourselves in and it is at this point, that you begin to transcend toward acceptance.

Dealing with our realities is considered the emotional side of this process, whereas acceptance is the physical side. Transcendence happens when we are able to not only acknowledge our emotions, but also take direct action to change those emotions. This combination is the rope bridge we all must cross in order to begin to improve our situation.

There are certain things that we obviously can't change in our lives, but we can work to improve them. Physical action leads to improvement. The first step is to simply accept the things we are unable to change. I have a chronic illness and I require kidney dialysis in order to survive. When I took the first step toward acceptance my life really changed. Anger and all of the other emotions on my list no longer consumed me. My perception of the situation changed and I realized that these emotions no longer had control. Hope took my hand and led me to acceptance, and acceptance gave me the ability to dream again. I began remembering an earlier time, a time before dialysis, and I thought about the dreams I once had.

The next step in the process of achieving acceptance is individual inspiration. We have to again ask ourselves the questions and seek out the answers. "How different would my life be if I did not have to receive kidney dialysis? What would be different in my life? What would I be doing with my time, and why would I make those choices?"

Inspiration leads to physical action and it is this implementation of action that allows us to gain **full** acceptance. An individual who is inspired can accomplish anything so this step in the process becomes very important.

I personally came to acceptance and individual inspiration rather quickly but was initially unable to implement both because of the mentally powerful hold that my emotions and experiences had on my life. It would be a decade before I was able to reach full acceptance and take physical action implementing what had inspired a promise to be made.

At age sixteen I was given information about my illness that would lead me on a journey of carelessness and self-destruction. Back then I was told that I was not expected to live past the age of twenty-five. So from that point on, every decision I made in my life was somehow colored by that information. This fatalistic view combined with a childhood of anger and every negative emotion that came with my diagnosis led me to make choices in my life that I may not have otherwise made. If given the opportunity, I would not change those choices because as individuals, we are the sum total of our own emotions/experiences and it's those things that define us, not control us. Acceptance has given me the wisdom to understand that difference and it is that understanding that has allowed me to separate my life from my diagnosis.

Living is the third and final stage and the stage where quality of life is achieved. Living is simply defined as the pursuit and achievement of our own personal goals and dreams. It is within this pursuit and achievement that we find substance, meaning, fulfillment, and overall happiness.

"Realize that you are more than your diagnosis and your perception will begin to change. Realize that you have goals and dreams, ask questions, seek answers, and strive to achieve. Your world will transform right before your eyes."
Shad Ireland 07/04

I offer **Deal, Accept, Live** as a road map to guide you along your journey as a dialysis patient. It is the formula I used to successfully change from an angry, non-compliant patient to the Ironman I am today. I have been successful because of that "road map" and I believe it will help you to successfully change your life as well, if you are willing to begin the journey. Take the first step; ask yourself the hard questions and seek the answers, reconnect with hope, take physical action, and accept the challenges in your life. To deal with where you have been is to grow, and to accept where you have yet to go is to take control and move forward.

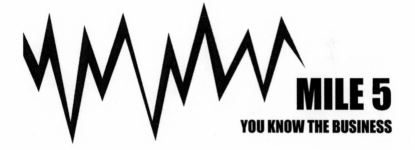

MILE 5

YOU KNOW THE BUSINESS

The next time I saw Troy was at the Rush. I was talking to a group of girls about a house party I was promoting that weekend when I felt a hand on my shoulder.

I turned to see who it was and I was greeted with a smile and a nod. "Sup Bro" he said. It was Troy. He had a girl on each arm. I winked and smiled. "Sup Bro, what's going on?" Troy reached into his pocket and pulled out a twenty-dollar bill. "This is for the party this weekend" He said. I took the twenty and told Troy the details. Both of the girls asked if they were invited, and Troy responded by asking them if they ever brought sand to the beach. That seemed to be all it took as both girls turned and walked away. He and I had a good laugh and turned to talk with the girls I was speaking to earlier. This was the superficial existence that we lived. This was Wonderland and in essence, the duality of my existence. All I wanted to do was party, drink, and chase girls, and all I wanted to have was an escape from my other life.

One of the first girls I met in Wonderland was named Joy. She was 5'2, 110 lbs with long brown hair, deep brown eyes, and a killer body. Joy approached me at a club called The Roxy. I had just walked off the dance floor after a contest when I felt a gentle touch on my arm. She smiled, introduced herself, and asked me where I learned to dance. I smiled back and without hesitation told her it came naturally.

Troy and a few other friends were standing with me and I gave them the look. "They knew the business." Joy and I grabbed a table upstairs in the corner. We talked for a long time and before we knew it, it was closing time. I looked around for all of my friends but lo and behold they were gone. Joy, seeing that I was now alone, looked at me and asked if I wanted to come back to her house. I smiled and said yes. How could I not... I knew the business. We went back to Joy's house, had a wild night and the next morning she drove me home. As I got out of the car I told her I would give her a call. I never did. You know the business.

A week later, Joy showed up at a house party I was promoting. Since I hadn't invited her I was surprised when she showed up. She gave me an evil look and started in with the questions. I had to talk fast, but of course within a couple of minutes she was laughing and smiling. I made plans to hook up with her after the party and all was right back in Wonderland.

Insanity is defined as repeating a particular action over and over while expecting to see a different result. With that being said, Joy and I got together after the party and had another great night. When the morning came we both got up and she drove me home. As I was exiting the car she reached over, grabbed my arm and said "You **are** going to call me right?" I of course replied with "Yeah, sure I will call you" I didn't call. I guess she didn't know the business after all.

A week went by and then one day a call came through. It was Joy. She asked if I had lost her number, so I lied and told her that I had not been feeling well all week. She asked me what I was doing that night and to keep up the pretence, I feigned a cough. That gave me my way out, so I told her I was staying in because I was still sick. She said if I wanted any company later to give her a call. I told her I just might do that. Then I hung up, glad that the conversation was over and I had managed to get out of seeing her, and called Tracey who was a dancer I had met at the mall a week earlier. We had been playing phone tag all week, so I was hoping this could be my chance.

In any event, I figured Joy was a solid back up if I could not get a hold of Tracey. That was the way my mind worked. I was always looking for something better, but with the notion that there was always something "acceptable" in the wings should what I really want, not turn out. I was pleased to hear Tracey answer after the first ring and we got right down to business. I gave her my address and she said she would be there in fifteen minutes.

About a half an hour later, Tracey pulled up in her new mustang. I got in the car and gave her a kiss. She reciprocated and devilishly asked me if I wanted to go over to her place and watch a movie. I smiled because I knew the business.

Tracey and I spent a few wild hours together. She was a few years older than me and had a gymnasts' build. She was in amazing shape. We stayed at her house until 1:30am and I had just started to doze off when she told me to get up and get dressed. I gave her a confused look and she smiled, telling me she liked to sleep alone; I guess she was showing me the business now, so I just laughed and got dressed. Fortunately for me she gave me a ride home, and as her mustang turned the corner onto my block my eyes nearly jumped out of my head. She pulled up to the front of my building and I could not believe who was sitting there. It was

Joy and she was holding a crock-pot filled with homemade chicken soup. Tracey leaned over and gave me a deep passionate kiss. Then, I got out of the car and told her I would call her later. As I shut the door and she drove off, I knew I was not going to be able to talk my way out of this one. Sure enough, I had to duck to the left as the crock-pot flew past my head.

Joy shouted a few expletives and ran to her car. What could I do? I was busted. I just smiled, shook my head, and went inside. I thought she knew the business, but I guess not.

In all seriousness, Joy was one of the few good ones and the way I treated her was wrong. I knew it at the time but at that point in my life I didn't care. I barely cared about myself so how could I care about anyone else. Joy called me a few days later and left several messages. She still wanted to get together, but I never called her back.

This was my life and all I wanted to do. Partying and chasing women was all I thought about and it consumed all of my time. I used these things to numb myself to the effects of dialysis. Getting high and partying with my friends helped me to get through the rough times. Well, that and the recreational acquaintances I was making did.

I remember the first time I went to dialysis after a night of heavy drinking. I showed up at the dialysis unit around 6:30am and you could smell the alcohol on me. I became belligerent and argued when the dialysis staff refused to perform dialysis on me. After several minutes the charge nurse agreed to put me on the machine. I think she wanted to teach me a lesson. Within a minute and a half of being connected to it, I became sober and quite sick. I began vomiting and begged for her to disconnect me.

I will always remember the look on her face and the smile she had as she disconnected me from the machine. I learned a lesson that morning: not to drink as much before dialysis.

Throughout this period of my life, I ran with a group of guys that liked to party. We promoted house parties and nightclubs in order to finance our collective lifestyles. They introduced me to the right people and I built a reputation rather quickly. We rode in limousines, drank the best liquor, and surrounded ourselves with the hottest girls. Even though these friendships were superficially based, I felt connected. All of us were rather competitive because the lifestyle was all about image. I was one of the first guys in our group to start using a limousine service to arrive at the clubs and parties we promoted. I successfully negotiated a monthly rate that was less expensive than a car payment and insurance, and when you added the image factor into the equation it worked out to be a great PR move. People began to talk, and that only enhanced my reputation. It also brought more people to the parties and clubs we promoted.

The first night we used the limousine service was a night I will always remember. Troy and a few other people were hanging out at my apartment having a few cocktails before we went out to the club. The buzzer rang and I told everyone that the limousine was here. Troy and a few others laughed and made a couple of comments. We all went down stairs, and to everyone's surprise, a stretched black Volvo limousine was parked and waiting in front of my apartment building. We all piled in and immediately began attacking the complimentary bar.

The ride to "The Rush" took about forty-five minutes and by the time the driver stopped the vehicle and opened the door everyone had a good buzz. Like a new bottle of Jack, out we poured. The line to get into the bar was quite long. There were about two hundred people waiting in line, but that didn't matter, we were known.

The bouncer lifted the velvet rope and motioned for us to circumvent the line. Troy slipped him the usual fifty-dollar bill and we proceeded to enter. As we entered, a voice shouted from somewhere in the back of the line. "Who do you think you are? The line begins back here." Troy looked at me and without missing a beat, gave the guy something to think about. "We are the guys who are going home with your girlfriend!" The entire crowd laughed and you could tell from the look on the guys face that he was embarrassed and upset. I was laughing pretty hard and was surprised when Troy began walking toward the back of the line and the object of his ridicule. I looked at the bouncer and we both began to walk after him. I thought for sure that Troy was going to knock this guy out. The next thing I knew he was standing in this guy's personal space talking to the girl that was with him and not paying any attention to the fact that this guy was only inches away from him. You could tell that this guy was quite heated but Troy just winked and smiled at him. What he said next was classic Troy. He had game. He looked deep into this girl's eye and said "You can stand in line for the next hour with him or you can VIP with us." I started laughing when the girl took Troy's hand and walked away. I thought for sure this guy was going to take a swing, but he didn't. He saved himself a trip to the hospital. Troy could handle himself in any situation. He always liked to push the envelope though. As he walked away with this guy's girl he looked at him and arrogantly said "You know the business." We walked back to the front of the line and into the club. The bouncer was a good friend of ours and about an hour later he made sure the guy was denied entry. We had a great time that night and after the club closed the limousine driver dropped both of them off at her house before taking me home.

I awoke the next afternoon to the sound of a ringing phone. I sat up and reached for the cordless. "Yeah, hello" I said. It was Troy. I asked him how last night went; he laughed and said, "You know the business." I told him to be at my house around 6:30pm and hung up. I was still really drunk so I had to lie down and fall back asleep for a while.

Troy arrived at my house around 6:30 pm and of course the first thing we did was sit down and talk about the girl from last night and laughed about how the whole situation went down. I went to the fridge and grabbed a couple of beers and when I came back into the living room Troy smiled and asked me if I wanted to get high. He reached into his pocket and pulled out a dub sack. It took a couple of minutes to separate the stems and seeds but neither of us was in a hurry. Troy rolled the fattest joint I had ever seen and passed it to me. "Spark it up" he said. I took the lighter in one hand and the joint in the other. I ran the lighter under the joint to heat seal it and put it to my lips. I lit the end and took in a deep breath. The weed cracked as I inhaled. We had missed a seed. I could only hold the smoke in my lungs for a few seconds. Weed smoke always tickled the back of my throat and burned my lungs. I began coughing and Troy smiled and motioned for me to pass the joint. "Rookie" he said. He grabbed it from my hand and took what seemed to me to be the never-ending hit. He held the smoke for a couple of minutes. I laughed and told him he could probably medal at the weed Olympics. He burst into laughter and began coughing. I looked at him as he caught his breath and held up three fingers. It was his way of saying "Pot, Kettle, Black". We smoked a few joints and passed the time as we waited for the limousine to arrive. Tonight we were headed to a club called "The Underground".

57

By the time the limo picked us up and we made the journey to "The Underground" we were really high. We were there to see a friend of ours who was the house DJ. His name was Tim and the music he spun was always good. Troy and I immediately headed to the bar where he bought a pitcher of beer and I bought six shots. Then we headed over to the DJ booth to say hi to Tim. The three of us stood there for a minute making small talk while we waited for the drinks. When they arrived we each did two shots and had a beer chaser. Then Tim went back to the music and Troy and I went to find a place to sit down.

Tim could make magic happen with a pair of 1200's. His specialty was beat mixing and it seemed like everyone we knew would always go to wherever Tim was spinning because he was that good. He could really move a party and everyone knew it.

Troy and I found a booth and took a seat where we continued drinking for about the next hour. As we did the boredom set in. I looked around the club, at the crowd, and casually said out loud, "Between the two of us I think we know everyone in here. This sucks, Minnesota sucks, the weather sucks, and the bars close too early. I need more, I need some excitement." Troy looked at me and said: "I know a couple of twins who are pretty exciting." I shot Troy a look because I was drunk and trying to make a point. He smiled and said "You know the business" which made me smile. I told him that I was serious and he nodded. "What do you want to do about it?" he asked. I knew what I wanted to do. I made one of those life changing drunken decisions. I told Troy that we were leaving, but before we left I ordered another round. We both slammed the shots and beers and headed for the door.

Troy and I headed upstairs and out into the blistering, blowing cold. We got in the car that was waiting for us and headed back toward my house. I told the driver to step on it as I looked at my watch and contemplated the decision I had just made. I tried to focus but the tequila was talking to me instead. We stopped by each of our houses, grabbed a few things, and headed for the Airport. We arrived with only a few minutes to spare. We both ran up to the counter just in time to make the last flight out. "Two tickets to LA please" I said. The ticket agent said that would be $3000 dollars. I smiled and started counting hundreds. We got our tickets and headed toward the gate. Troy looked at me and shook his head. "You were serious back at "The Underground" weren't you?" he asked. I looked at him and responded "I wanted to see the ocean before I died."

We boarded the plane and settled in for a three and a half hour plane ride. I awoke to the sound of our plane touching down in Los Angeles. I was excited. The city with all of its lights beckoned. We headed outside the terminal and looked for the shuttle to the rental car company. I took in a deep breath and held it for a moment. I felt alive. The excitement was hard to contain. I looked at Troy and thought to myself, this is great. We are standing in Los Angeles with no contacts, no reservations, and no idea of what we were going to do next.

This is what made it so exciting. This to me was living. We boarded the shuttle bus that took us to the rental car company. I was hoping that they wouldn't notice the fact that we were drunk. I sat back and enjoyed the ride, not worried at all. I knew if there were a girl behind the counter we'd have no problems getting her to rent us a car.

Troy and I thanked the girl behind the rental counter and promised that we would give her a call later. As we walked out into the parking lot Troy crumpled the piece of paper with her number on it and tossed it onto the ground. We both laughed and jumped into the convertible Mustang. I dropped the top and started the car. The engine roared to life and true to its name, the car began to gallop.

I lit a cigarette and watched as the city with all of its colors went passing me by. Troy reached over from the passenger seat and turned on the radio but all I could hear was the wind as we sped along on the freeway. Troy reached over and tapped my shoulder, which suddenly brought me back to the moment. Until then, I had been busy taking in all the visuals. He started talking about this club ad he'd just heard on the radio and said we should head to Hollywood to check it out. I nodded and smiled. "Hollywood it is then" as I put my foot down on the accelerator and changed lanes. I wanted to see what the car could do, and here was my excuse to find out.

We drove around until we found the club. Fortunately for us we also found a parking spot in the club's lot. I parked the car and we jumped out. The line outside was quite long and if there was one thing we were not accustomed to doing, it was waiting in line. As we stood, you could hear the energy permeating through the walls. I began to rhythmically nod my head to the beats that were coming from inside, and as I looked to my right Troy was already putting in work. He had struck up a conversation with this brunette, and her red headed friend was smiling at me. We talked with the girls while we waited for the line to move, and when we finally got to the front, the biggest bouncer I had ever seen was standing in the doorway checking ID'S. He looked down at me and asked me for mine. "Minnesota, you are a long way from home" He said. "What brings you to Hollywood?" "Your club" I responded. I told him that we had just grabbed a flight and were looking to party. He laughed and asked "How many?" I looked over at Troy and noticed that he was making progress with both of the girls we had just met. I told the bouncer "four" as I pointed over to Troy and the two girls. The bouncer said that would be a hundred dollars. I asked him if that was the tourist rate. He was not amused, and responded by asking me what we paid in Minnesota for cover. I told him that we never pay a cover because we (as I motioned to Troy and myself) are known. The bouncer began laughing and said "I like you Minnesota, you are all right." He stepped aside and all four of us walked in without paying the cover charge.

The club was bigger than anything I had ever seen before. There must have been over a thousand people partying and having a good time. The dance floor was packed so we headed to the bar. Troy ordered a round of shots and we officially began drinking again. He held his glass up and said, "May your liver last longer than mine."

After finishing the shots we took the brunette and the redhead out onto the dance floor. We were all having a good time when both Troy and I noticed a circle forming in the middle. We grabbed the girls and headed deeper in to check out the circle. It was a phenomenon all its own; a place that you either shone or looked foolish. Both Troy and I could hold our own in the circle and we knew it. It was a great way to meet women. We both incorporated our personalities into our dance moves and had a way of moving the crowd. Troy was very good at break dancing and I had a unique rhythm that mixed a lot of different styles. Troy beat me into the circle and I watched as he did a few steps I had never seen him do before. I nodded and followed after him. As we were dancing, I noticed this kid watching from the other side of the circle. He was nodding his head and taking visual notes. I finished by popping up on my left foot (ballet style) and spinning. It looked good with the strobe light effect. I left "Center Stage" and smiled at Troy. I noticed several people in the crowd staring. It felt good to get recognition and acknowledgement especially considering the talented dancers that were showcasing in the circle. One of those dancers was the kid who I noticed watching us. His name was LA and he had some moves that rocked the crowd. He came over and introduced himself, asking where we were from. We told him Minnesota and continued the conversation at the bar.

We were talking to LA when I heard the bouncer call my name from the far end of the bar. "Minnesota" he shouted. He came over to all of us and asked if we were interested in going to an after party. Both Troy and I were game so the bouncer wrote down all of the pertinent details. At the top of the napkin he wrote in bold letters, BRING AN EGG!

My memory gets a little hazy at this point. I only remember bits and pieces, fragments really. I am surprised that I **can** remember anything at all because we were both on a steady infusion of alcohol and drugs. What I can piece together now seems like a bad trip but at the time seemed rather normal (well normal for Wonderland anyway).

I sat in the car and waited for Troy to come out of the Quickie Mart. As he stumbled through the door he held up his right hand and showed me a single egg. I laughed and yelled "Finally!" This was the fourth place we had gone to on our quest to find that friggin' egg. It apparently was the key to the after party so of course that meant we had to get one. It was like the secret knock or the password; if we had the egg, we were golden. We had driven all around Hollywood and finally found the prize. Now it was time to REALLY party.

The crowded Hollywood streets were filled with nameless faces, and I watched as those faces melted away while we sped by. The bass from the radio and the music of the street put me into a trance like state. I was in a world of my own and was quite enjoying it when all of a sudden I heard Troy yell, "RED LIGHT!" I instinctively slammed on the brakes and the car came to a screeching stop. You could smell the rubber from the tires. Troy looked at me and asked, "Are you good bro?" "Yeah, I'm good... Good and drunk" I responded. "YOU KNOW THE BUSINESS!" We both laughed as we waited for the light to turn green.

We drove by the place a couple of times before we realized it. So I flipped a u-turn and pulled into a dark parking lot next to the building. I am not sure how we found it at all, given our condition. It all seemed like a strange dream as we exited the car, lit cigarettes, and headed toward the side of the building where the door was located. The last memory I had was of Troy and I getting into an elevator. I remember how it shook from all of the bass. From there I guess I blacked out. Hours of my life disappeared and they were gone forever.

I awoke the next day and panic immediately set in. I sat up and looked around horrified because I had no idea where I was or how I had gotten there. The memories of the previous night's activities actually came back to me after about two weeks. I was confused and in a strange hotel room with my friend Troy who was passed out on the couch across the room. I saw the phone on the night stand and dialled the operator. "I would like to make a collect call please." I gave the operator the number for my parent's house and my mom answered after the second ring. "Collect call from Shad, will you accept the charges?" asked the operator. "Yes, I will accept the charges" she said. I could tell from her tone that she was mad. She immediately asked, "Why are you calling me collect? Where are you?" "I am not really sure, I am in a hotel room." I responded. "A hotel room? You were out drinking with Troy again weren't you?" Yeah, I was. I held the phone in one hand and pulled the curtain back from the window with the other. I told my mom I did not know where I was and that I was looking out the window at palm trees. (It was winter in Minnesota). "WHERE ARE YOU!?" She screamed.

I noticed our airline tickets on the desk and after taking a quick look I was able to figure out where we were. I told my mom that we were in LA. She asked me how we got there, and when I told her we took a plane she was not amused. When I look back on it now, I think I called her because she was always a stabilizing force in my life. When things were bad or I was confused she always made me feel safe. My mother's voice helped me to get my bearings and I told her I would call her when I got back to Minnesota.

I wanted to get off the phone before the lecture began. "What about dialysis? You can't miss treatments" everything I didn't want to hear at the time, but everything I of course needed to hear. Troy and I ended up hooking up with the girls from the night before again and spent the next couple of days partying in LA before making our way back to Minnesota.

After getting back home I continued to party and run with the same group of friends. Months went by and I flirted with the idea of change occasionally, but I had this predominant belief that I was going to die before I reached the age of twenty-five. All I knew was that my doctors had given me what I thought was a death sentence and I was doing what I could to speed the process along. I would fade in and out of Wonderland and spent many hours alone in my apartment struggling with the duality and craziness of my life. On one hand I was fearful and angry about an illness that I had no control over. I did not want to die. But on the other hand, I was consuming copious amounts of drugs and alcohol to numb the emotional pain and hide the scars from a childhood that left me feeling detached and without any real connection to myself, or the world around me.

At this point, I was again feeling suicidal. For years I felt like I was in the passenger seat watching my life careen out of control. It was during these long hours in my apartment that I came to understand the need for the duality and craziness I'd experienced in my life. It was all about control; not only the lack of it that I had back then, but how important it would be for me to use those experiences to gain the control back.

MILE 6
THE TRANSPLANT

The first couple of years I lived in Wonderland was exciting, but the lifestyle, like my illness took its toll. My general outlook on life and the way that I treated everyone correlated directly with how I was living and how I perceived my situation. Wonderland warped my sense of reality, accelerated my carelessness, took my humanity, left me feeling even emptier, and then it took my soul. Its contributing affects only accelerated my inability to accept my situation and my interactions with the real world became even angrier. I turned to Wonderland to escape from reality, to find fun and excitement, but the excitement I initially found eventually became more painful than the life I was hiding from. If there is any true lesson I learned from those experiences at that time in my life, it's that.

At the end of the night I still felt empty inside. I was angry and afraid, and I knew I was losing control again. I couldn't consume enough drugs and alcohol to maintain the numbness. It had been what I'd turned to in the past, but now I found myself realizing that it wasn't a savior, but instead something temporary to mask what I was not wanting to deal with. Sometime during the day, within each twenty-four hour span, I would emerge from Wonderland to find myself confronting reality and the medically fragile state of my existence. The impending loss of control again coupled with the duality of my existence led me back to a very scary place. It was a place filled with darkness, hopelessness, and despair. In other words, I was in Hell. I was standing on the edge, looking into the abyss, contemplating suicide again, but a conversation with a stranger would impact my decision that night and take me back to a simpler time filled with truth and faith. A place where life used to make sense and God existed.

As a child I often attended church with my brother and mother. It was at an early age that I initially came to believe in Jesus Christ. It was this belief that instilled in me the existence of God and things greater than ourselves, or the world we occupied. I watched as my mother endured years of physical and emotional abuse, spousal desertion, and financial hardships, but her faith and belief never wavered. My brother and I both endured similar abuse, and while his faith was a source of strength, by the age of eleven I began to question mine. My childhood perceptions grew into questions that had no answers and prayers went repeatedly unanswered. As a child I once believed that we were all God's children, that his love for us was unconditional. But through the abuse, desertion, and medical illness, God the father, like my biological father, did not exist to me.

I spent years feeling empty inside. The darkness from within led me to question my existence and the reason for it all. I was suicidal. I left my apartment late one night and wandered around until I eventually found myself sitting on a park bench. I had my face in my hands and I was distraught.

It was dark, quiet, and I'd thought I was alone, but suddenly a voice from out of nowhere asked if I was all right. I jumped about three feet in the air because I didn't notice that a man had come and taken a seat next to me. I was too consumed by thoughts of my life and what to do about them. Again the voice asked if I was all right. I looked at this man and tried to fight back the tears, but everything just came pouring out. I began to cry and ended up talking to this stranger for a couple of hours. I can look back now and say that his words and advice truly saved my life. We talked about my childhood, my illness, and how I struggled with addiction. Then he asked me if I knew of Jesus Christ. I responded by laughing and told him how faithless I had become. He challenged me to reconnect with hope, and to rediscover my faith. He told me that God was listening, and if I prayed he would answer me.

As I walked home I kept replaying the conversation I had with the stranger in my mind. I thought about what he had said and how he looked me in my eyes and told me that God was listening. I scoffed at the thought. I walked into my apartment and immediately began swallowing pills. Who was this guy trying to kid? I knew what I had to do. I'd decided I wanted it all too finally end. I couldn't take the craziness any longer. I have no memory of how many pills I swallowed that night, but I do remember that I quickly began to feel sick. I raced for the bathroom and began to vomit. I felt so sick that I thought about calling for an ambulance... but I didn't.

I hugged the toilet and wretched so hard that I began to hallucinate. My mind drifted as my head slumped into the toilet bowel. Wonderland was not the fun and exciting place it used to be. As I slipped in and out of consciousness I found myself standing alone at the Mad Hatters table with overturned chairs and disorganization everywhere. I looked to my left and watched as the beautifully colorful garden wilted and died, and the surrounding green forest turned dark and imposing. The trees became ominous as the darkness closed in. I could tell the end was coming.

There was no end though. Instead, I awoke to find dried blood in my nose and on my face. It hurt to move, and I was lying in a pool of my own vomit at the base of the toilet again. I was not sure how long I had been there or even what day it was. I wasn't sure about anything really, except that life this way sucked, and I couldn't stand the thought of having to suffer this much for another day. My head hurt and I had this strange memory about being on a park bench talking to a stranger. His voice kept playing in my head, "God is listening, if you pray he will answer you." I picked myself up off of the floor and stumbled over to the shower. I sat in the shower fully clothed and let the hot water run over me.

I was a mess, but eventually stood up and took my clothes off, reached over, and threw them into the garbage can by the door. Meanwhile the stranger's voice kept getting louder and clearer in my mind: "God is listening, if you pray he will answer you."

I finished taking a shower, crawled into bed, and then began to cry. I was afraid, alone, and at the end of my rope. Without any hope, and what felt like nothing left, I made a decision and began to pray, asking God if he remembered me.

That entire week I was incredibly sick. My body was trying to recover from all of the personal abuse I'd put it through and I was paying for it. Between all of the drugs, booze, and pills I took to OD I was lucky to be alive, yet I didn't feel that lucky. Instead I was a mess both physically and emotionally. It would be the events that followed that would allow me to begin to reconnect with hope and begin to rediscover my faith. It began with a phone call.

March 12th, 1990

The phone rang and it was my mother on the other end. I looked at the clock and it said 4:00pm. Her enthusiastic energy was contagious. She yelled through the phone "We have a kidney!"
I didn't know how to respond, except that I could feel my heart skipping a couple of beats. My mother began giving me instructions and when she was done I told her I would meet her at the hospital. My mind was spinning as I contemplated the thought of no more dialysis. I honestly thought I was going to be cured, so I jumped at the chance for a new life and ran as fast as I could to the hospital.

As I ran the excitement and anticipation grew. I was feeling positive about my future for the first time in many years. The emotional and physical chains that bound me to the monster were being removed and I was going to run as fast and as far away as I could. I was going to be set free!

This new sense of freedom scared me though. I had as many negative thoughts as I had positive ones. What if I had complications from the surgery? What if the kidney didn't work? What if they decided I couldn't have the kidney? As I entered the main doors of the hospital I was sweating and shaking from the adrenaline rush and it was hard to breathe. I got in the elevator and pressed the button for the fifth floor. I was barely able to contain myself. I had to report to station 5C. The transplant clock was running.

The hospital received multiple organs that day and every patient that received a phone call was riding that same emotional roller coaster. We each had more questions than answers but we all shared the same euphoric feeling. I could see the anticipation in the eyes of the other patients who were waiting as I walked into the waiting area for 5C. It was amazing to be surrounded by so much happiness and excitement. You could tell from our faces, we were each about to receive the ultimate gift, the gift of life.

As I sat in the waiting room with the others I read the checklist I was given upon arrival. I needed to have my blood work drawn for a test called a "Type and Cross", and an antigen match. I needed to have what I hoped would be my last dialysis treatment, and I needed to read a book and watch a few videos that would educate me about the transplantation process and the aftercare required. Everything seemed simple enough and I was more than eager to get to it.

I never believed that I would ever receive that phone call. As I thought about it I shook with nervous anticipation. This was going to be a life-changing event that I would liken to winning the lottery. The excitement and disbelief was overwhelming. Transplantation has that type of immediate impact on the recipient.

I quietly watched as the other organ candidates were taken to their perspective rooms. My left leg bounced up and down as I sat in this small uncomfortable chair. I got up several times and paced around the small waiting area. While I did, I asked myself "When will they come and take me?" My mind was racing.

I watched as the nurse slowly approached and when our eyes connected she smiled. "Come with me please Shad" she said. So I followed her down the hall. She took me to my room and showed me my bed. On it was a robe, a gown, and a book on transplantation. I was given several instructions and told to immediately change into the gown and robe. "You need to hurry" she said. Then she left the room and I changed into the patient uniform. A few minutes later I was introduced to one of the transplant surgeons, the person from the lab who came to draw liters of my blood, someone from the transplant office also came in and introduced herself, and several others who comprised the team arrived to assure me that my transition into my new life would go smoothly.

I was overwhelmed and in awe, but ultimately incredibly happy to be in the position I was at that moment. I was being given a second chance, a new start, and this time, I would do it right.

Try to imagine your life about to instantly change, but you have to wait twelve hours for that change to begin. Then try to imagine, there still being a possibility of that change not happening. It all came down to the blood tests. So I had to wait twelve more hours. After that, I would find out if I were going to be free.

My last dialysis treatment seemed surreal. I looked around the unit for what I thought would be the last time. It was well past 11pm before the treatment began so it was quiet. As I watched the blood leave my body I noticed the other empty chairs and the dialysis machines next to them. The mechanical monsters did not look so scary now. I thought about the other kids who were not so lucky. I remembered their struggles and the empty stares from across the room. We silently supported each other as the monster took our blood from our bodies and returned it with a little less life than the minute before. We knew we were all dying and that emotional and physical drain was enormous. The tears began to roll down my face as I sat there quietly and thought about the other kids who never got this chance. I felt guilty because a week earlier I had tried to commit suicide. I felt guilty because I truly didn't feel that I deserved this gift. I made poor choices, was combative and generally non-compliant yet here I sat, given this chance at freedom. That night I quietly promised the ones who did not make it that I would take this gift for them and do whatever I needed to do. I would change. I had to change.

Some of the people who comprised the transplant team had reservations about me. I did not have the best reputation. Many of them thought that they were wasting an organ on me and questioned whether transplant was a good decision.

Although I did not know it at the time, others went to the mat for me. They fought to make sure that I was given this chance. When I later found out I was humbled.

After the transplant I wrote a short letter to the family who made the difficult decision to donate. I struggled with what to say, as I was only given bits and pieces of information. I was told that a woman in Florida lost her son in a motorcycle accident. One mother took her pain and loss and gave another mother hope again. How graceful and selfless. I couldn't be more thankful.

I now have the words that I struggled with years ago.

Wherever you are I want you to know how thankful I truly am for what you have given me. Your son's tragic end gave me a new beginning; something I never expected to have in this lifetime. Even though I would eventually lose your gift due to complications beyond anyone's control, it continues to live on in spirit. The decision you made to donate your son's kidneys saved my life and allowed me to become the man I am today. The positive impact I am having in other patient's lives now is a direct result of that gift. Your loss grew into something greater than simply giving me my life back. It now gives hope to others who are struggling with this illness. Your son continues to live on through my accomplishments and will continue to do so after me through the lives of the patients who I reach everyday. Thank you.

My mother came running into the dialysis unit around 4am with a great big smile on her face. She screamed, "We have a kidney!" She was holding a copy of the blood test results and they were positive. The kidney was a match. Things began to move rather quickly after that. So many people were involved in making this happen. They were like a well-oiled machine; a transplant assembly line. They had procedures to follow and things were being marked off of the checklist one by one.

At 6am I was being wheeled down to the third floor. This was where the operating rooms were located and where all the magic would happen. I was shivering under the blankets and tried not to bite my tongue as my teeth chattered. I was afraid but smiled through it giving everyone we passed thumbs up and telling them

I was getting a kidney transplant today.

The operating room always had a distinct smell whenever you entered. The cool embrace I felt as I entered always sent chills up my spine. One thing I have always liked about the operating room was the blanket warmer. I immediately requested three blankets and one of the OR nurses brought them right over. Even though I'd had numerous other surgeries before receiving my transplant the gravity of my situation hit me as they were transferring me from the bed to the operating table.

I began to experience claustrophobia and tried to take deep breaths. Both the operating room nurse and the nurse anaesthetist noticed my discomfort and took steps to distract me. Within a few seconds we were talking and laughing. A minute later I faded to black.

Beep, beep, beep, beep, beep, "Shad?" "Shad, open your eyes" "You are ok; you're in the recovery room." "Ahhh" I moaned and reached for the oxygen mask that was covering my face. My right side hurt badly and I could not focus. I passed ou…

The next brief memory I had was when they brought me back to my hospital room and transferred me back into my bed. I was in a lot off pain and swore several times during the transfer process. It took six people to complete the transfer process. I had two IV'S, a pair of Nemo-boots (these are used to help with circulation and to keep blood clots from forming in your legs after surgery), an oxygen mask, a heart rate monitor, and a Foley catheter in the bladder. I looked great and I heard the good news before I passed out again. The kidney began working on the operating room table.

"Shad, take a deep breath." "Huh?" I mumbled. I opened one eye. The nurse put a mouthpiece with a plastic tube connected to it in my mouth and told me to inhale. "You have to take a deeper breath!" Her voice was stern so I figured I better do what she said and inhaled deeply, but it hurt badly. "Come on Shad, deeper" she said. So I took a deeper breath and began to cough. I remember the nurse smiling at me before I passed out again.

This was my routine for the next few days. Wake up, roll over, sit up, get out of bed, stand here, walk to me, walk to the door, walk down the hall, I just wanted to sleep. Didn't these people realize I just had surgery? I was in quite a bit of pain and also out of it from all of the pain medications.

My family was of course there through it all. They were as excited as I was. Every time I opened my eyes someone was there with me and I was greeted with a smile. My mother took every step with me. I could only imagine how hard my illness had been on her and how scared she must have been for me. She was smiling brightly as I took my first few steps after surgery. I remember her grabbing the Foley catheter and pointing to the urine in the bag. "Look Shad, you're peeing" she said. She always had a way of making me smile through it all.

After about a week I regained my mobility and the pain had subsided. I was walking up and down the halls of the hospital and getting stronger with each step. As I walked I spent a lot of time thinking about how my life had changed and how lucky I was.

I thought about where I had been and the condition I was in just two weeks prior. I kept thinking about that park bench and the stranger I had met. His words continued to ring in my head like church bells. "God is listening, if you pray he will answer you." One of the first places I went after regaining my mobility was the hospital chapel. I sat in this beautiful room and thanked God. He was listening, and remembered who I was. The night that I broke down and prayed I asked God to take the yoke I was carrying because the weight was unbearable. I challenged him to reveal himself. I prayed, "If I am one of your children and you truly love me you will help me." A week later I received a kidney transplant. Some people would call this a coincidence but I cannot deny the truth. As I spent time in the chapel I reflected on these things as well as my youthful rebellious past.

I thought about how my childhood was filled with so much pain and anger, and how kidney failure left me physically and emotionally beaten. I was without faith for so many years and now I had come full circle. Faith is like hope; it is the knowledge of, and belief in a better life. Unfortunately I would again face future challenges with both.

The kidney began rejecting shortly after my third daily visit to the hospital chapel. It began mildly but would take a severe turn rather quickly. I was also experiencing side affects to the immune suppressive medications. My mood became erratic and I rapidly gained weight (this was caused from the high doses of steroids given to help suppress the immune system) I had fevers and pain that I never experienced before. I retained water and my blood pressure skyrocketed. My body was heading for a civil war. It would begin with a few small uprisings that were quickly put down, but as one battle was finished another would begin. Each battle became fiercer and all out civil war was on the horizon.

One of those battles left me decimated. A virus called CMV was attacking me. The virus attacked my entire body and made it almost impossible to move. The pain was unbearable. I was bed ridden for over a week. Each day that the battle raged it became bloodier than the last, and it looked like my position would be overrun. But when the smoke cleared and the dust finally settled I was left standing.

On many occasions I would receive my discharge papers but tensions would rise and battles would again break out all over. I would find myself being repeatedly hospitalized. It seemed my body was not going to accept the terms of surrender and there simply would be no foreign occupation. My body considered the kidney to be an invader so it mobilized its armed forces and battle after battle ensued.

ALG was the weapon of choice. This drug was used to treat acute rejection episodes. My generals would come to my hospital room and discuss the war plans. We would repel each new attack with ALG but the casualties were mounting. The kidney and its function could not continue to withstand the war. We were winning the battles but quietly my generals thought it was only a matter of time before the war would be lost.

I fought as hard as I could and took my medicine as I was instructed, but the war took its toll and I became weary. I struggled on many occasions both physically and emotionally as I heard stories of other battles. There seemed to be a pattern. Patients who would stop taking their medications would lose their transplanted kidney. That was not going to be me. I would have rather died than to accept defeat and find myself back on kidney dialysis, back in the jaws of the monster.

Each battle took me emotionally back to when I first received my diagnosis. I was struggling, and physically I was losing the war. Darkness was setting in and I could hear the monster howling in the distance. I remember the day the transplant team entered my hospital room and began to prepare me for surrender. I flashed back to when I was a ten-year-old child. How I sat there and held on tightly to my mothers arm. I was not that child anymore. I was a veteran, and I would not accept surrender. If I were to go down then it would be fighting. I asked the team if we had anything left in our arsenal. We did. They told me of a new weapon that was still experimental. Its name was OKT3. I signed the required releases and began a seven-day course of the drug that afternoon.

We dropped the bomb around 4pm. The drug was injected intravenously and my arm became hot as it seemingly exploded. The impending battle was going to be fierce and I prepared myself as the other side began its counter attack. My body convulsed and I began to spike a temperature. I vomited repeatedly and slipped in and out of consciousness. The battle raged for over a day and a half and when I awoke from it all I was left with nightmares. I had no fight left.

When the nurse entered my room to administer the second dose of OKT3, I raised the white flag. I was ready to surrender. I could not endure another battle. "The worst is over, I promise" she said. It took a few minutes and some encouragement from her to convince me to continue to fight. I received the second injection of OKT3 and the side effects were mild in comparison. A few days after completing the seven-day course of the drug I received my final discharge papers. I had 70% function in the transplanted kidney and my lab values normalized. The war was over.

My friends and family were happy to see me come home, as they had witnessed it all. They were there and supported me through the entire process yet I still felt alone and disconnected. I had no idea what I was going to do with my life; I had no discipline or direction. Emotionally I was in pieces. I still had not dealt with the addictions, abuse from my childhood, or the anger I felt. I had years of frustrations buried deep inside of me. Troy and I would get together sometimes and talk about moving away from Minnesota. We talked about traveling to Europe and backpacking, we reminisced, then we talked about partying all over the world. Now I could do all of those things. I was free, right? Nope. Emotionally I was still chained to everything from my past. And I was chained to my illness too. The dreams I'd had for my life after transplant quickly faded. I was afraid to live. I was afraid that I would have another rejection episode, and that my illness would come back.

This fear is called "survivorship". It's fear of the unknown and not knowing what to do next. At least with kidney failure I knew what I had to do. Three days a week I reported to the dialysis unit. I needed dialysis in order to survive. Over the years, kidney failure and the required dialysis treatments defined my existence. This was my life and all I knew. So what was I supposed to do now?

I would wake up at night screaming. I'd had nightmares about the monster. He was chasing me and I had nowhere to hide. I spent days just sitting in my house waiting for the transplant to finally fail. I should have been joyous but depression set in. I was paralyzed by fear.

While I was battling to save my transplanted kidney my mother met an angel. His name was Bob. I now call him dad. At the time, I had a deep distrust for men and was very protective of my mother. I treated Bob like I would have treated my biological father if he were around, yet Bob responded with love. I was not his son but he came to the hospital to visit me. He was a rock for my mother. A shelter from the storm. He supported both of us through it all and even tried with my mother to encourage me to go to college. But I believed it was only a matter of time before the monster would have me again.

Bob is a strong, quiet, soft-spoken man who truly loved my mother and treated her like I had never seen anyone treat her before. At the time I didn't understand. What was his angle? There had to be one. Why was he so nice to my mother? Why did he act like he cared? I was sure he would be abusive. In fact I was convinced of it.

I remember the happiest day of their lives. My brother and I were at our mother's house and both she and Bob walked in through the garage door. They were holding hands and smiling like two teenagers in love. My mood and attitude immediately changed as they both stood in front of my brother and me and smiled widely. "We have something we want to tell you, we are getting married" they said. I had never seen my mother so happy. For years she spent countless nights alone in her room after working two jobs reading a book until she fell asleep. Some nights I would hear her sobbing. Then Bob came along and filled those nights. He made our mother feel special and told her that he loved her every chance he had. But instead of being thrilled and elated that my mother finally had a true and deserving man in her life, my response was venomous. I looked at them both and said "SO WHAT" and stormed out of the house saying that I did not approve. As I passed my mother I saw tears in her eyes. Clearly my response was not expected and it hurt her deeply. Bob considered not marrying my mother because of what I'd said, as he did not want to come between us. I am so glad that he decided differently. I'm a better person because of Bob and my life would not be complete without my dad. I love him.

You see, at the time I didn't trust Bob. I was incapable of trusting anyone really. I was sure he was up to something and that he would eventually hurt my mother. I was stubborn and it broke my mother's heart. I remained that way until a few days before their wedding. I gave them both a letter and I watched as my mother read my words and tears rolled down her face. Both she and Bob gave me a hug.

In that letter I apologized and explained why I acted the way I did. I wished them happiness and told them that I loved them both. They were married for a total of thirteen years before my mother lost her life due to lung cancer. She was only 56 years old. She was terminally diagnosed as I trained for the Ironman in Lake Placid, but that story I will save for a later chapter.

MILE 7

ONE THE ROAD AND A PROMISE MADE

My transplant lasted a total of three years. Regrettably I never took advantage of the opportunity I had been given. I never went to Europe with Troy. In fact I rarely left my house and when I did people would stare. The reason was because I suffered from body image issues. I didn't like myself and felt trapped; dealing with what physical cards had been dealt to me as a result of gaining my life back.

One of the drugs I needed to take was called Prednisone. This drug is a steroid and has multiple side effects. All transplant patients get what is called a moon face and develop cheeks like a gopher. I got that face and also developed bad acne. When combined with the 55lbs of weight I had gained after the transplant I struggled to find the energy to leave my house.

Another of the drugs I was taking was Cyclosporine, and one of its side effects is uncontrollable shaking. I remember being in a restaurant and trying to hold the menu steady. The waitress asked if I was all right. She obviously thought I was having a mild seizure, but I tried to make it seem like nothing, and told her I was fine.

Receiving a kidney transplant was not the cure I had expected. It was another form of treatment, and as it turned out this treatment had complications just like dialysis. Once again I wasn't happy. The euphoria had worn off, and one more time I became depressed.

I feel that before I continue I need to clarify a few things regarding transplantation. Personally I have decided not to attempt another kidney transplant. I have had two which have both failed. My body doesn't tolerate the side effects from the immune suppressive medications. Unfortunately I am one of those patients who are in the 5% patient category that has severe reactions due to the transplant medication. I **am** however in favor of transplantation. I have seen the miracle work for other patients and I believe that everyone needs to be an organ or tissue donor. In many ways, as I discussed in an earlier chapter, the transplant I received saved my life!

Over the three-year period I had my transplanted kidney I struggled with the side effects from the medications and other personal issues. Medically I was still fragile. Fear was such a predominant factor in my life for so long that it became an unwanted companion. I longed to be free and it seemed I wasn't quite there yet. I still didn't know how to deal with my reality and struggled to come to terms with the fact that I traded one form of bondage for another. The options were death, dialysis & transplantation.

This is the reality for anyone who has kidney failure, and this reality was too painful for me to accept. That is why I went back to Wonderland. That is why I abused substances before, and once again.

I found that I spent the majority of my time either at home or at the hospital and I watched as two years of my life passed me by. I felt like I was going nowhere and every morning I would wake up and fear would be there to greet me. It was a lonely time in my life. I missed all of the action in Wonderland, so I picked up the phone and called some old friends. I dove head first down the rabbit hole again.

When I arrived back in Wonderland it didn't surprise me to see Troy seated at the head of the table. It was his turn to be the Mad Hatter. So he raised his teacup and toasted my return. We shared a joint and talked about old times. We even talked about leaving Minnesota. It felt really good to see him again. I looked around the room and noticed a lot of familiar faces; the characters were the same, the only thing that had changed was where they were seated at the table.

After we finished smoking the joint I asked Troy for a cigarette. The first puff was tough, but like every other bad habit that night, it came back real easy. I got up from where I was seated and headed toward the bathroom. I had to pee. As I walked through the house many of my old friends showed me love. It felt good to be back. I felt connected again.

The next morning I awoke to find myself sprawled out on my bed. I was face down and fully dressed. I didn't know how I had gotten home. I guess I must have blacked out again. I looked over at my nightstand and smiled. Troy left his calling card. There was a lighter with four cigarettes, and a note that read
"You know the business."

I got up and took my morning dose of medications, then headed to the bathroom to take a shower. I let the water run for a minute before I entered. It felt good to get the smell of smoke off my skin. I thought about the night before and started to smile. Then I heard a noise in the background and turned my head. It sounded like someone had walked in my house. So I turned off the water, grabbed a towel, and got dressed. I came out of the bathroom and was surprised to see Troy sitting on my couch. "Sup bro, your front door was unlocked so I let myself in." He was rolling a joint. I grabbed a seat on the couch and turned on the television. He handed me the joint and I raised my hand. "I'm good" I said. Troy shrugged and took a hit. "Last night, were you serious about getting out of Minnesota?" he asked. "Hell yeah," I responded. He asked me where I wanted to go, so I told him I was thinking about California. He told me he wanted to move to Florida. We sat and talked for about an hour, played dice, and laughed about the old times. Before he left we had decided that we were going to get out of Minnesota; and not just a spur of the moment trip like our last escapade. This time we decided we were going to move.

I finished loading up my van and closed the door. I turned back to look at my house and shook my head in disbelief. I could not believe I was moving. It was only a week earlier that I went back to visit Wonderland. It was only a week earlier that Troy and I talked about moving. As impulsive as it was, I felt good about the decision. I thought a change would do me good. My parents had no clue I was leaving, and I wouldn't share it with them until I arrived at our destination. They were used to me arbitrarily taking off like this so I figured this time would be no different.

We had no jobs, no contacts in California and a few thousand dollars between us. We didn't even have an apartment lined up. I thought about everything and shook my head. I laughed and jumped into the driver's seat, looked over at Troy and said, "California is going to be great." He smiled, nodded his head, and we were off.

We left Minnesota around 7pm. Troy agreed to drive through the night so I pulled over at a rest stop somewhere in Iowa so we could change positions. I looked at Troy and told him to take a right on interstate 80. "Right on 80 got it" he said.
I climbed into the back seat and proceeded to fall asleep. Troy ended up driving for the next twelve hours. As I opened my eyes and rubbed them, I saw that the van was stopped at a red light. I looked out the window and saw "the golden arches." Troy took a left into the parking lot, parked the van, then turned to me and said "Bro, I need a coffee."

I jumped out of the van and looked up to the sky. It was beautiful; crystal-clear blue, and not a cloud anywhere. I had absolutely no idea where we were so I asked Troy "How far did we make it?" "Where are we?" He smiled and replied "Colorado I think?" I looked around but didn't see any mountains. So rather than try to figure it out, I walked in to McDonalds and did what everyone does. I stared at the menu for a couple of minutes. The woman behind the counter asked, "Sir, can I help you?" I guess I had a surprised look on my face because she proceeded to ask me if I was all right. I was stunned. I thought I'd just heard a southern accent. I asked her where I was and turned sideways to look out the window at Troy. He was leaning up against the van, saw me looking at him, and waved and smiled. The woman behind the counter seemed puzzled by my question. "Sir, you're in McDonalds" she responded. I shook my head and said, "I know that, what state am I in?" I was getting frustrated. I was still half asleep. "Sir, you are in Tennessee" I shook my head and laughed. The woman behind the counter gave me a strange look and asked if I was all right. I ordered breakfast and took it to go. I walked out side shaking my head. As I approached the van Troy smiled and said "Bro, you are going to love Florida" I handed him his coffee and said, "I guess we were moving to Florida all along." He smiled and shook his head. "You guessed right."

We ended up in Fort Meyers Florida and after about a month we ran out of money and had to get jobs. I spent six months working as a bus boy and hanging out on the beach. I made $4.25 an hour plus a meal at the end of my shift. I lived on barbecue beef for about six months. Money was tight but I made enough to get by. I eventually got tired of Florida. I hated my job and thought about going to school. I called my parents and they convinced me I should move back. Bob still had his house by Lake Nokomis and told me that I could live there if I went to school. The invitation was too good to turn down so I sold my van and grabbed a flight home. Troy stayed behind in Florida for awhile and then once he got tired of it he moved on and traveled around the country, only to eventually wind up back in Minnesota a couple of years later.

It took me a few months to get settled after getting back to Minnesota. I eventually registered for spring classes but I was preoccupied with other things. I lacked the discipline college required. It would be a few years before I was ready to take college seriously. I seemed to be walking through life with my eyes closed. I was living for the moment, devoid of hopes and dreams and I still had no direction. I smoked weed and drank to numb the pain. I could not get motivated which only fed my depression. It wasn't long before I withdrew from all of my classes which made my parents upset. As a result, we argued because I felt like they just didn't understand. As time wore on our relationship became strained.

I didn't want to go to sleep at night so I would drink and smoke until I passed out, but that didn't seem to help. I kept having the same nightmare. I was in the woods and it was dark. I would hear howling in the distance. It was after me, the monster. He was coming for me. I tried to run as fast as I could but seemed to be running in place. I looked over my shoulder and I could see his fangs. Then I would wake up covered in sweat screaming for my life.

These nightmares continued off and on for several weeks. I had the same one for years. I wasn't sleeping much, and generally I was starting to feel run down. I began to feel sick but I assumed it was because of the lack of sleep. After a few days the headache I had remained constant and Tylenol had no effect anymore. I thought I was catching a really bad case of the flu. I knew things were bad when I woke up one night shaking. I was covered in sweat from a fever. My temperature was 102.9 and climbing. I lifted my shirt because I had pain over my transplanted kidney. I noticed the skin was discolored and hot to the touch. I tried to sit up but felt dizzy, and my head was pounding. I felt like I had to vomit so I reached for the garbage can because I knew I wasn't going to make it to the bathroom. I was in trouble. I tried to walk to the bathroom but collapsed. So I crawled to the kitchen and grabbed the cordless phone. I knew I was dying. I reached for the phone and called 911. "Help Me," I cried.

As I laid in the emergency room barely breathing, I slipped in and out of consciousness. Civil war had broken out again and this time I was going to be the last causality. My body was in full rejection and I was rapidly deteriorating. The nurses and doctors had so many questions but I could not breathe. Tears filled my eyes as I watched all the commotion that was going on around me. I tried to speak through the oxygen mask but my voice cracked and gurgled because my lungs were filling with fluid. The nurse who took care of me was so beautiful. She touched my forehead softly and told me everything would be fine. Another nurse was trying to explain to me that I needed to sign a consent form so that they could insert a tube into my lungs to breathe for me. I guess I'd had a living directive that said I refused any life saving measures. One of the nurses knew my mother personally so she called her to get consent.

My mother told her to go to me and explain the situation, to tell me that I had to sign a release. It felt like I was slowly drowning. At that point I would have signed anything. My mother arrived at the hospital emergency room twenty-two minutes later but I was already in ICU. I was being besieged. The battle was not going well and I was in a full on retreat. With nowhere left to run I turned and fought as best I could but they were attacking with everything they had. My body was taking a pounding. I was battered and bloody. It didn't look good.

The doctors explained to my family that my body was shutting down. I was rejecting the transplanted kidney which was secondary to the fact that my lungs were continuing to fill with fluid. I showed physical symptoms of a massive brain tumor but scan after scan came back negative. I had some of the best and brightest taking care of me yet they didn't have any definitive answers. My family was distraught and my mother broke down after the team of doctors told them that I would not make it through the next twenty-four hours. Later, she would recount the entire story to me. Apparently, she ran her fingers through my hair as she did when I was a child. After a few minutes she bent over and kissed me on my forehead and choking back the tears she said goodbye. My mother left me that afternoon expecting never to see me again.

When she got into the elevator it all came out. She broke down and began sobbing. Bob tried to console her but she continued to weep. The elevator doors opened and my mother looked up to see a face she had not seen in years. It was a face from my childhood. It was Michael Garr. He used to be a counsellor at Wilder; now he was a Doctor of Cardiology. He recognized my mother right away and asked her what was wrong. She told him of the dire circumstances I was in, and the terrible news she had just received about my impending death. He immediately took her back to ICU and got involved with my care. He promised her that he would personally do everything he could for me and that everything would be all right.

The next part of the story she told me was really rather strange because my biological father had shown up out of nowhere, and was standing in the room watching me when my mother arrived. She was shocked to see him so she asked how he found out that I was there. He never answered her. Instead, he did what he'd done so many years before, and just walked out.

I spent six weeks in and out of a coma. When I'd first entered the emergency room, I weighed 145lbs. I awoke to emaciation.

When I opened my eyes I saw its fangs in my arm. I thought I was having a nightmare so I tried to close my eyes and make it all go away. I wanted to wake up but I held my eyes tightly shut because the sound was all too familiar. It had been three years since I felt its bite and heard that sound. It was the sound of the beast. I was connected to a dialysis machine again.

That night after being wheeled back to my room I decided to take a shower. I was weak and felt dirty. I had no real concept of the situation I was in or the battles I had recently lived through. At the time I had no memory of the last six weeks. All I knew was that I always felt better after a shower so I swung my legs over the side of the bed and tried to stand up. Unfortunately for me, my legs didn't work. My muscles had atrophied so I crumpled to the ground. I tried to stand but my leg muscles felt like they were on fire so instead I just crawled to the bathroom. I was determined to take a shower. I braced myself against the wall and used the handrails to hold myself up. I turned on the water and waited a few moments as I've always done. Then I disrobed and entered the shower. I looked at my naked body and began crying. I could see my hipbones and my rib cage. I picked up a bar of soap and franticly began scrubbing. I tried to wash it all away. So many years of uncertainty and fear came rushing back at that moment. I became overwhelmed and fell to the ground sobbing. I sat in that shower for over an hour and cried. I felt like I was ten years old again and very afraid. I wanted my mom. I felt alone so I asked God if he was still listening.

How many times would I turn away from God? How many times would I ask for forgiveness? How many times would I find myself in this situation? Would he give me another chance? It would have been easy to raise my hand in the air and curse him, or to let fear and anger continue to rule my life. I couldn't deny the truth. That truth was that my lifestyle had put me there. I always took my transplant medications but the lifestyle choices I made put me in that shower. I will always remember that shower because it was at that point, my weakest point, where God gave me the strength to continue.

By embracing the truth I found my strength, but fear and anger were not quite done with me yet. I left the shower feeling drained. I crawled back into bed and slept deeply. It would still be several weeks before I was discharged from the hospital and many of the doctors and nurses thought I would not last six months.

Those first six months of recovery were brutal. I had no energy and spent almost all of my time lying on my mother's couch. My routine consisted of sleeping and going to dialysis. I could barely eat and had no appetite. There were many times when I just wanted to die. I was back to feeling hopeless and did not even have enough energy to be angry. Now it was a struggle just to find the physical strength to sit up.

I spent a total of thirteen months on my mothers couch recovering and it was one of the most difficult times in my life. The following quote is one that I feel really defines this period of my life. It's one that made sense to me then and makes sense to me now, so I always have it with me in my thoughts whenever there is an obstacle in my life to face. *"An individual cannot know their truest ability until they are faced with great adversity"* –*UNKNOWN.*

What happened next would be a mile marker, and the first of many defining moments in my life. It would be a decade later before my life would truly change but I can tell you that it was this moment that the seeds of change were planted.

I came across this story about an amazing group of athletes. Triathletes they were called. They were doing this race in Hawaii called the Ironman and I immediately fell in love. Hawaii was amazing! It reminded me of California. I told my mother to come and take a look. I pointed to the TV and told her I was going to move there. She asked me what I would do for a job and I told her I would sell beaded necklaces on the beach. She laughed. "Maybe when you get better you can do that" she said. I sat there mesmerized by how beautiful the scenery was. My mind drifted until I heard the announcer talk about the distances. "The Ironman consists of a 2.4 mile swim, a 112 mile bike ride, followed by a 26.2 mile run." I was amazed. The first thought I had was how could they do that? The next thought I had was that I could do that. It was at that moment that my future would be determined. It was at that moment that I made a promise to myself. I decided that one day that would be me running with the best athletes in the world. I told myself that I would compete in the Ironman World Championship. It was at that moment that a promise was made.

I fell asleep that afternoon dreaming of Hawaii. One moment I was in the ocean swimming, beautifully blue and crystal clear, the next moment I was riding a bike, my race number flapping in the wind. I was in awe. Moments later I felt this intense burning pain in my legs. I was running, but it was so hard to put one foot in front of the other. Everything was in slow motion and I could feel my chest rubbing against the fabric of the jersey I was wearing. My ears were filled with the steady rhythm of my breathing. It kept cadence with each step as the sweat dripped off of my forehead and ran into my eyes. I turned my head from side to side and watched as the crowd cheered me on toward the finish line.

Suddenly I sat up and looked around the living room. I was dazed and half asleep. My mother was sitting in her chair and asked me what was wrong. I looked at her and half mumbled, "I was there, I was there." She gave me a confused look and shook her head. Then she told me to lie down and go back to sleep, so I did. Within a few minutes I was sleeping again, dreaming of what I had decided would be my future.

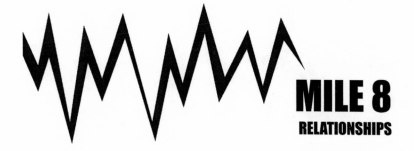

MILE 8
RELATIONSHIPS

As I said earlier in the book, universally we all experience the same emotions and those emotions contribute to our experiences. It is through these similar experiences that we are able to find connections and out of those connections grow relationships. In this chapter I wanted to share a few words with you about some of my relationships and the impact they have had on my life.

Sean

I have not talked about my brother very much up until now. He and I are very different people but he has always had my respect and love. We have become quite a bit closer after losing our mother. When I was younger I hurt my brother as I hurt my mother, but like her, he always responded with love.

Sean is a testament to unconditional love. He has been a role model and a light when the darkness surrounded me. He recently shared with me that in previous years he thought I looked down on him. That was never the case. My brother is older than me and I have always looked up to him, but I could never find the right words to say. He looks a lot like our mother. I have told him this on many occasions. Kindness, gentleness, and understanding are just a few of the qualities they both shared. Sean has also taught me spiritually. He has led by example, answered my questions, and continues to be a guide on my walk with Christ.

Troy

What can I say that has not already been said? He has been my friend through it all. We have shared the good times and the bad. Troy is like a brother to me. We are family. You know the business!

Dan

I met my friend Dan many years ago. He could tell you stories about me. He was there when I was in ICU fighting for my life. He is a teacher by trade and someone whom I have had many debates with. I respect his intelligence.

Our friendship is unique and has had many incarnations. Dan, like Troy has been with me through it all. He is like a brother to me. Over the years he has questioned some of my choices and his advice has caused me to take pause on occasion. This is what friends do for each other. For many years while I struggled with Wonderland and its addictions Dan chose education. Dan and I would hang out and talk, but for years I think he believed that I was not listening. That was not the case. He always encouraged me to pursue education and his educational success made an impression.

One of the reasons I have such a strong drive to give back and make a difference in the lives of others is because of his actions. I have never told him this, but watching him work with kids and getting involved with his community gave me ideas. Our actions seem to always be observed by others and those actions have the ability to impact us in ways that we can't even imagine. Dan's ideas have manifested into the success I am seeing with my foundation and for that I will always be grateful.

Andrea

A few years ago I needed a friend and she was there. When few people believed in the vision I had for the Shad Ireland Foundation she supported that vision.

So much so that a lot of the success we have had is because of her dedication. She has played an important role in the development of Team Ireland and was instrumental in the expansion of my foundation into Canada. She is the Executive Director for the Shad Ireland Foundation Canada and together we have worked very hard to see the successful implementation of that vision. She has been one of the few people I have confided in. She was also one of the few people I turned to when my mother died. Andrea is an amazing woman who I deeply respect and admire. Her loyalty, commitment, and dedication to my vision of making a difference in the lives of those affected by kidney disease has made a significant difference in mine.

Team Ireland 2006

Team Ireland started off as an idea I had at 3am. I always refer to them as a tool because the attention we gain from having that group of athletes race for us, does nothing but increase our opportunity to help others. I know that by continuing to race I have the ability to inspire other dialysis patients, but what about those who don't have kidney disease? Will they be inspired by my story? Again my hope is that Team Ireland will be the tool that will bring attention to everyone, kidney disease patients or not. Then word will spread and our success will grow to the point where we can continuously help patients gain back their lives.

I believe the overall message is so important because there are millions of people who are affected by chronic illness and millions more who are terminal. It is so easy to turn to anger, fear, and frustration when you're in that position. When I found my way out of that darkness I was a changed man.

In college I learned many things. One of those things came out of a question a professor posed to me. He asked me what I thought about my education. He asked me if I thought that getting an education was a gift, and if so, do I feel a responsibility to give back to others in return for this gift. The conclusion I came to was that I have a responsibility to give back to others. I took that question and applied it to the many different aspects of my life. I realized that my illness was not a limitation. I have been given so many gifts. That same professor also gave me a book that changed my life. That book was "Tuesday's with Morrie."

Whether we are healthy or we suffer from a chronic or terminal illness, we all share similar emotions. These emotions contribute to our experiences and it is through similar experiences that we are able to connect with others; this is how we develop relationships and how we grow. This was how I came up with the team message of **NO LIMITATIONS ONLY INSPIRATION**.

Team Ireland consists of healthy and challenged athletes who believe as I do, in the power of inspiration. That inspirational power that you see in the Ironman triathlon lies in its essence and simplistic beauty. The race is not about the external distance or environment. It is about the individual's internal struggle.

All you could ever expect of yourself was that you gave everything you had when that moment came and you were faced with the ultimate challenge. It is about celebrating life and every breath along the way. It's not about being the best it's about being the best you can be.

Even though triathlon is considered an individual sport, I believe that together we are stronger as a team. Each of us will approach the starting line individually but complete every race as a team. Together we will not only inspire others, but make a difference to everyone we touch. In ourselves we see each other, and in our own shared reflection we see that essence and simplistic beauty. As I developed Team Ireland the main questions I had were would others be inspired by my story? Will they join me in promoting the message? The following essays from my teammates answered those questions. These people have joined me, and others continue to join us on a daily basis. I have become friends with each athlete on my team and our relationships have developed over the past year. We have all become closer because of those same emotions and our similar experiences. I look forward to working with them as we strive to affect as many kidney dialysis patients as we can and give them as much of their lives back as possible.

Nick

After hearing about your team and how there are no limitations just inspiration, I knew I had to be involved! At a very young age, I have been exposed to the medical world. Growing up, my father was an OBGYN and my sister worked in the pharmaceutical industry. Ever since high school I have known that I would be involved in the medical arena in some capacity. For the past 8 years I have been working in the pharmaceutical/biotech industry. It is a great feeling to help so many people with wonderful medications/treatments that are available. At times, I feel like a physician, as I have become a specialist in many disease states over the years; everything from Asthma, Migraine, Seizure, Depression, Flu, RSV, Cancer, and now End Stage Renal Disease. Shad after listening to your story, you are truly the reason that I am out there each day working with physicians and staff to make sure that education and access to life changing medications are available. On my first call to a dialysis center, I could not wait to tell your story to continue motivating social workers and dieticians that they are the patients advocate and we must do everything possible to help these patients have a better life! I believe that you have inspired so many with your Lake Placid IM accomplishment and your quest to someday race in IM Hawaii. Last year I also completed my first Ironman in Lake Placid, NY.

Competing in Lake Placid that same day I can understand and relate to the emotions that you must have had. It is all about the fight to keep going to accomplish your goal, set new barriers, and prove the doubters wrong. It is also nice to hear the words "Shad Ireland you now are an IRONMAN" You have shown so many that regardless of your situation you need to live life in the fullest, and take advantage of each day! I would be honored to be apart of your TEAM!

Jeff

I have been in Healthcare for over 16 years and in the Dialysis business since 1999. I have seen the many challenges that Dialysis patients face and our company works very hard to help them in many ways from providing innovative treatment options, laboratory values, to funding many new NKF initiatives.

I have also been involved in Triathlon since 1989 doing over 100 Triathlons of varying distances and recently completed my 2nd Ironman event at IM Florida. Once I met Shad, I was 100% sold on the ideas and dreams he has for himself and the foundation. I am fortunate enough to be able to compete and race in this great sport and have made some life long friends along the way. It is the shared experience of training and racing that makes us all "teammates" in some way. Just to get to the starting line is a HUGE accomplishment for anyone and one that binds us all.

My goal is to help Shad and the foundation in any way I can, through racing, fundraising or spreading the word of passion and success to anyone who will listen. This is a great opportunity to help the people within the Dialysis community and others with chronic diseases and to show them all that although they have a disease, it is only a limitation, if they allow it to be one.

Chris

On December 3rd, 1995 I ran my first marathon. At the time, I was 20 years old and a junior at the University of the Pacific. Just two days later, I was diagnosed with Cancer. Some people define themselves by what they do for work, what they drive or what sport they compete in. I define myself as a cancer survivor. Having survived Cancer is something I am very proud of. It may sound a little dark, but having two major surgeries, undergoing months of chemotherapy and living with the knowledge that my life could be over in a matter of months completely changed my outlook on life. Having Cancer changed me into a better person. I know how lucky I am and I try to live my life to the fullest. Since being placed into remission 9 years ago, I have dedicated myself to helping those who are living with Cancer. Whether it is talking to chemo patients in my doctor's office or raising money for charity, I feel like I have an obligation to help those who are fighting the disease. When I was first diagnosed, I was an avid runner and was just beginning to train for ultra-endurance events. Some people run for health reasons or as a way to lose weight. Running was much more than that for me. Running was a part of who I *was. Running kept my life in balance and was something that was completely my own. While visiting doctors across the country to determine a treatment strategy, I asked them each about the effect the treatments would have on my desire to continue running and competing in endurance events. While each doctor recommended a different treatment strategy, they all agreed that I would never be able to race endurance events after undergoing the intense chemotherapy treatments. Their assumption was that the damage to my lungs and other internal organs would be too great. The way they made me feel, unfortunately, was that there "was no life after Cancer." While in the hospital at the USC-Norris Cancer Center, I promised myself that I would run the same marathon the following year and would compete in an Ironman Triathlon within five years. I also decided that I would raise money while competing in these events to help build awareness that Cancer survivor's could have their lives back following chemotherapy. Not only did this give me a goal to look forward to during my treatments, but it also allowed me to transform my body from that of a sick chemotherapy patient to one of an athlete once I was placed into remission. After months of chemotherapy and surgeries, I was placed into remission and my quest to reach my goals began. On December 5th, 1996 I ran the same marathon again and finished it 10 minutes faster than the previous year. I finished the Ironman Canada Triathlon in 2002 and haven't looked back since. Ironman is considered one of the most difficult sporting events in the world. Consisting of a 2.4mile Swim, 112mile Bike and a 26.2mile Run, the Ironman Triathlon took me almost two solid years to train for. In the end, I finished the race in just over 12 hours. But, best of all, I was able to raise over $20,000 and help generate awareness for Cancer Survivors. I continue to train and race for Ironman Triathlons and marathons across the country. I dedicate each race to those are affected by Cancer and am constantly looking for new ways to spread my message that there IS life after Cancer.*

Pia

This past year I have had to face some of the best and most difficult times in my life. I not only married the man of my dreams, I lost my mom to cancer and finished my first Ironman all within a short period of two weeks. My husband, Chris, has been my inspiration behind triathlons, and once he got me started I have developed a love for the sport. In fact he would say he has created a monster. He is celebrating his 9th year in remission since he was diagnosed with testicular cancer. He has taught me a lot about life and living it in the moment. Let me start off by saying that my family and friends thought I was crazy to do an Ironman just two weeks before my wedding. I began to train for Ironman Lake Placid and plan our August wedding when I received a call from my mom telling me that she was diagnosed with stage 4 lung cancer. It was almost unbelievable. I had so much running through my mind I really wasn't sure what I was supposed to do. Do I call off the wedding? Can I commit all of the hours to training for Ironman? Since I was a little girl I imagined all the planning and fun of a wedding. I certainly hadn't pictured the challenges I was about to face. But, one thing stuck in my mind throughout the tough times was to never give up. My mom was the strongest person I knew and she always told me I could do anything. I continued to support my mom in the challenges of chemo, train, live everyday life and with a lot of help from my husband, plan the most memorable day of our lives. I have to admit it was tough. Getting back from a 7 hr bike ride and then rushing off to try on wedding dresses without my mother. I couldn't help but to feel guilty not being with her all the time. Being a teacher I had the summer off and was able to be home with her. In June the cancer had spread to her brain, spine and to many of her vital organs. She was in the hospital for months and then we were able to bring her home, which is where she wanted to be. The summer went by and with my mom hanging onto life, I was faced with the tough decision to leave for Lake Placid or not. It isn't an easy decision when all of your family members can hardly believe I would leave my mom in this state to do a race. But as I sat by her bed side and looked down at our LIVESTRONG bands, I knew that I had to go for myself and my mom. Ironman was a truly amazing experience. You really have a lot of time to think about life when you are alone for almost 13 hours. I knew my mom was out there with me cheering me on in spirit. I finished with a huge smile on my face and I immediately told Chris to sign me up for another one! I was back with my mom now with my wedding less than two weeks away. I had known for a while she wasn't going to make the ceremony. I couldn't believe I was going to have to get married without my mom. Again it was so hard to leave her side, and somehow I knew she would be there with me again and as I kissed her goodbye, I knew it was going to be the last time I saw her before she passed. This past year I have learned that life isn't easy, we are all faced with challenges and we have a choice on how we want to approach those challenges. With the strong drive and determination my mom has instilled in me, and the inspiration I have from my husband I choose to go for it all and give it my personal best. It is sometimes scary to say it, but I live everyday as if it could be my last. Living life to its fullest is

*one of the reasons why I want to become a part of Team Ireland.
There are few people in the world who actually live their lives to
the fullest. My goals is to become part of a team of athletes who
love the sport of triathlon and work together to inspire others to
reach for their dreams and never give up.*

Denile-
*In 1979 I was diagnosed with obstructive renal problems that,
despite surgery, lead to kidney failure at the age of 26 in 1997.
From a very young age I was aware that my time here was a
gift and that I should not waste a moment. My first experience
with dialysis lasted 9 months. I was the fortunate recipient of a
living-related transplant. During my first experience with dialysis
I continue to teach group fitness and exercise. After my 1997
transplant, a gift from my wonderful brother (he still gets props),
I decided that life on dialysis was restrictive and I was going to
enjoy every moment of freedom I had. While I was on dialysis the
first time I made a list of everything I wanted to accomplish and
there were no limits to what I could write down. The list was not
bound by money, time, health, or reason. At the time it was just an
exercise to keep me focused on the positive. It was only in looking
back years later that I realized I had accomplished nearly 70% of
my list. I competed in triathlons, earned my CSCS certification
as a trainer, earned my Wilderness First responder certification,
became a white water guide, and rode as a cross-country team
rider with Girls on the Move (a special project of Outward Bound
International). I was fortunate enough to get to do lots of great stuff.
I lost my transplant in Jan. 2004 for reasons no one could explain.
One doctor joked that maybe being too healthy was my problem. I
was shocked to find that this time I am stronger than I was on my
first go round with dialysis. I believe that there are no excuses for
limiting oneself. I think optimism and sheer strength of heart win
out over diagnosis and disease every time! I believe that people
should be purveyors of health and well-being. I have spent 10+
years paddling white water rivers, puzzling at challenging climbing
routes, hiking up and down unforgiving mountains, running and
cycling across anything that would have me, and swimming until I
thought I would grow gills. I always tell my fitness clients that their
body will always give them more than their brain will. And I have
always been most inspired by those individuals who met their
challenges head on and with humor. A 13.1 mile run seems small
in comparison to a round of radiation and chemo. I know what it
means to be tired and ready to quit. But I also know what it means
to sit in a chair for 4 hours three times per week. My experiences*

have taught me to believe in myself and my ability to accomplish the things I fear I can not finish. I think these experiences will give me something to draw on as a 2006 team member. What I know for sure is this... as individuals we make choices everyday about how we will use our time and treat ourselves and others. Health is a point on a line and with every choice we make we are moving directly towards it or directly away from it. As a wife, mother, sister, and friend, I have a passionate, genuine interest in discovering how I can help others make good choices about their health and in what motivates people to make the choices they do. This interest has taken me back to school to attempt to earn a PhD in health psychology and hopefully one day conduct research that will help change lives. I think people should know that they can be healthy despite diagnosis. I hate that most people would consider me to be unhealthy, because despite my kidneys not working, I'm fine. I hate that some consider me to be disabled. I'm perfectly capable of doing everything but peeing. This actually makes me better at long car rides because I never have to stop unless I want to stop. Every experience as a member of a team is different and I anticipate the need to be flexible, generous, forgiving of others and oneself, and to keep a sense of humor. I am privileged to be surrounded by people who are supportive and courageous in their own lives. I am continually renewed by the stories that others share about what drives them to achieve their goals. Shad's story brought me hope and a renewed sense of determination that I am grateful for. Thanks Shad.

Mia
Each day I look for opportunities to make a difference in this world. For this reason, I chose the nursing profession. I obtained my RN license in 1998 and worked in the Neonatal Intensive Care Unit at UCLA Medical Center for one year, and then joined a traveling nursing program which gave me the opportunity to travel and work in Hawaii for a period of four years. While I was there, I participated in my first marathon. I played competitive sports (softball) from the age of seven until college, and I was involved in running. During my time in Hawaii, I had no idea what an Ironman was until a friend of mine asked me to volunteer in the medical tent for the Hawaii Ironman event. I was so inspired by the incredible distances those athletes had to indoor, and I was amazed to learn there were athletes out on the course with disabilities. I was so intrigued by there ability to overcome the impairment. I wanted to participate with these individuals, and I got on line and learned about a San Diego based non profit organization called The

Challenged Athlete Foundation. Approximately six months later, I moved to San Diego and immediately got involved in the sport of triathlon. I've participated in two half Ironman distance races in my first year. The first was California Half Ironman, and the second being Auburn International formally known as the "World's Toughest Half". I will be competing in my first Ironman distance race next April at Ironman Arizona, and I will be participating in the triathlon challenge with the challenged athletes in October 2005. I believe I would be a valuable asset to the team. I'm an individual who is dedicated to their career and enjoys helping others. My career provides the opportunity to help families with children born with an illness or disability. When a child is brought to the hospital, one of my responsibilities is to make sure the family understand the disease process and help them to learn better coping skills by education. The nurses are at the bedside 24 hours a day providing support and encouragement and helping the families to believe their child will survive. When an infant's life is in our hands, the family needs our support and inspiration to fight the battle they are facing. My aspiration is to set the same example with people who want to accomplish the same goals. When I complain about how hard life is sometimes, I find comfort knowing that I have the determination and will to fight and not give up. It's important for me to reach my goals with other people sharing the same experience. I wouldn't have been able to complete my accomplishments without the support of my friends and family. We can do this together by inspiring one another to accomplish our goals. I believe in what Shad said "Together we are stronger and together we will not only inspire, but make a difference.

Josh

I've been a sufferer or Crohn's Disease since 1991. At that time I had emergency bowel surgery that involved the removal of a good part of my intestines. The problem with Crohn's disease is that even when you cut out the bad parts, it never goes away. My doctors have promised me that should I live a normal lifespan, I will without a doubt undergo several more surgeries. I started doing triathlons six years ago. It has been instrumental in helping to slow the spread of the disease. At the time I did not think that it would be possible to finish a sprint triathlon. 6 years later, I just finished my second half-ironman. It was during the gruelling last 8 miles on the run at the Backwater Eagleman that I met Shad. It was amazing to me that there was someone else out there who was doing triathlons just to prove to themselves (if not the world) that it could be done! I have always believed that with the right focus and mindset - d reams and goals could be achieved. I wanted to prove to all sufferers of Crohn's Disease that they could successfully live a normal life and even complete an endurance test like a half-ironman. Previously I served as the President of the Central Ohio Chapter of the Crohn 's and Colitis Foundation where I tried to show the world that it was possible to get a law degree and an MBA while having Crohn 's. Now the challenge is completing an Ironman triathlon. Like Shad, I have wanted to be the first sufferer of Crohn's to cross that finish line on a full Ironman. The challenge with Crohn's disease is that it afflicts so many people when they are in their teens. It is a particularly difficult time to be faced with a potentially life threatening disease. My hope is that finishing an Ironman will provide hope and encouragement to those who may feel down and out as a result of having Crohn 's because of all the life limitations that the disease places on people. Selfishly, I would also like to prove to myself that I can do it. Much like Chris Crichton, triathlons have brought a sense of balance to my life. It provides me an outlet to channel my stress away from my stomach and into something creative and productive. In that sense triathlons have become much more about a lifestyle than a race. Why else would anyone go for a run in the pitch black darkness at 6AM on a freezing February morning? My new motto - "No limitations - only inspiration!"

Scott

I have been racing triathlons for the past 4 years and have found the sport extremely inspirational and motivating in my everyday life. You hear about folks that have challenges and race triathlons, but you rarely get to meet these individuals, until I met Shad at a local bike shop. His story and pursuit of his goals have inspired me to be a part of this team. In everything I do in life I remember one quote for me that I read in Lance Armstrong's biography "Pain is temporary, quitting is forever".

Shad and his team epitomize this philosophy by not only racing, but by making a difference in the community helping others to do the same by the Shad Ireland Foundation.

This past year has been my best yet as I won my first race ever at the Oakdale Duathlon in Oakdale, MN, second overall at the Tinman _ Ironman in Menomonie, WI, 1st place in my age group at the Lifetime Fitness Triathlon, which has all been the building blocks to do Ironman Wisconsin September 11th 2005. Although it was 95 degrees with 20mph sustained winds, considered the worst conditions with the highest did Not Finish (DNF) rate in Ironman history, I would not have changed a thing. Because of persistence and support of family and friends I was lucky enough to finish 4th in my age group, 42nd overall, and qualify for the Hawaiian Ironman Championships in October of 2006. I look forward to the challenge and only hope that Shad fulfills his dream, and is racing there with me. See you in Hawaii!

Nicholas

Growing up I've always loved and participated in a variety of sports. Soccer was my passion and my dream and I routinely took part in international tournaments and tours in Europe. At the age of 15 I was invited to a select training camp in Hungary to be scouted by European clubs. A month before I was scheduled to leave, I was hit by a taxi cab and broke my leg just above the ankle. After a year and a half of rehabilitation I tried to return to the sport but become prone to constant injuries around my ankle. For a few years I was depressed and then my life long best friend died in a car crash, I was at the lowest point in my life. They say when a door closes another opens all I know was that I was determined to open another door myself. My mother and my aunt had been competing in triathlon for years, I had never really paid it much attention but my mom had just gotten a bronze medal in her age group at the World Championships (my aunt capturing gold), so a year and a half ago I decided to give it a try. I think one of the greatest things about the sport is the people and the more I was exposed to multipart the more I was inspired to compete and perform as an athlete not just for myself but hopefully to inspire others myself one day. I'm on my way winning my first local Duathlon, as well as finishing 2nd qualifier in my age group and now getting the chance to compete for Canada in the 2006 age group World Duathlon Championships. When my father told my about Team Ireland the more I found out, the more I knew I just had to be a part of it. Its stories like Shad's that have inspired my through my first year in multi-sport. Joining something like this is not just an opportunity to push myself to reach my goals through friendship, and support, but to hopefully give back to the community and live out a dream inspiring others to live out their goals the way I myself have been inspired.

On a more personal level, I have dated quite a bit. I have loved very few women in my life, and even fewer were allowed inside my walls. As a matter of fact I can count them on one hand. My illness, and the fear, anger, and pain I felt from losing the ones

I allowed inside only strengthened the walls that allowed me to keep others at a distance. One of those women told me that it was because she didn't see a future with a sick man while a few of the others were not so cold, they just couldn't hide what was obvious. This for me was one of the most painful things I have had to experience in my life. Why was I not good enough to be loved? I couldn't change the fact that I was sick. This was the subject of the discussion my friends and I were having over lunch one day. I was telling my friends, Tom and Lori about what we as patients experience when it comes to personal and intimate relationships. I was telling them about a woman I had recently met. I was telling them about Roxanne and why she was so different and amazing.

Roxanne-

I met Roxanne during my 2005 race season. She was not like any of the women I had ever dated. Roxanne is quite a bit younger than me and her choice of professions surprised me. She is an Operating Engineer. She operates heavy equipment for a construction company and loves her job. I would see her after work occasionally and ask her how her day was. She always responded by saying "It was great." Eventually I became frustrated with the same three-word answer and so she elaborated. "The day that my job is no longer great is the day that I quit." Her response made me smile. What perspective she had, I thought. We spent many late nights talking on the phone and in person. Both our schedules were so busy that when we got time to spend together it seemed to go by too fast.

Roxanne has a large family and she is from Northern Minnesota. I on the other hand, grew up in the inner city of St. Paul and Minneapolis. Our differences endeared us to each other and quickly I started feeling very comfortable with her.

I normally didn't tell the women I dated that I was on kidney dialysis. I had grown tired of the explanations, questions, and eventual failure of the relationship due to my illness. I was content to date and have fun, and so strategically I planned on not having that type of relationship ever again. Roxanne was different though. I got lost in her eyes and taken by her smile. It's one that can brighten anyone's day, and when she does she has a way of looking at me that makes me feel like I am in second grade again with a schoolyard crush. She makes me laugh and is one of the most caring people I have ever met.

I remember the day I told Roxanne about dialysis and why I needed it in order to survive. She knew what it was. I was surprised. Then she informed me that she was in the Army previously and that her job was as a combat medic. She had a way of continually surprising me. I gave her the specifics and told her that I did home dialysis. She had a ton of questions but they seemed genuine and not based on fear. I told her about the machine, the process and procedures, and what it took to do dialysis at home. She was excited. She wanted to see the magic happen. I was startled. I smiled and told her I was not that type of guy. "I did not do that on the first few dates, dialysis is a commitment." We both laughed. I love that about Roxanne. We spend a lot of time laughing.

"I remember the first time she told me she loved me." I paused for a moment, considered what I was going to say, and looked Tom and Lori in their eyes, "It takes an amazing person to want to love someone with a chronic illness." I said. I reached for my glass of water and took a long drink. There were several moments of silence as we sat outside finishing our lunch on a beautiful summer afternoon. I was in Madison Wisconsin for the Ironman. I was there to support Dr. Tom Pintar in his pursuit of the Iron dream.

Tom
Tom and I have become good friends over the past couple of years. He is someone whom I deeply respect and admire. Both of us share a mutual passion for triathlon and he was one of my first supporters. He followed my training schedule via my website and sent me encouraging emails.

What I was attempting to do at Lake Placid was a source of inspiration for Tom, so much so that I received an email from him with the following announcement: "I registered for Ironman Wisconsin!" I was so moved by what I experienced that day that I wrote the following and posted it on my website.

I awoke to a high pitched sound coming from the alarm clock. I turned my head to the right and looked at the red numbers, 4:15am. As it was before every race, my stomach was in knots. I sat up and rubbed my eyes while yawning and taking a deep breath. I scanned the hotel room looking for my pre-race bag which normally contained a juice box, instant oatmeal, a couple of GU packets, and a blueberry muffin. This was my Ironman routine. This was race morning. It took me a minute before I was fully awake and realized that today I would not be competing; that today I was in Madison to provide support and encouragement for my friend Tom. Tom heard about my foundation, the Shad Ireland Foundation, and wanted to get involved. Through the Janus Charity Challenge, and private donations, he was able to raise over $13,000 for the foundation. One person racing with purpose, surpassing physical limitations, giving back, inspiring everyone he knows, and making a difference in the lives of others. This is the essence of an Ironman triathlete. This is why I knew that after today, Dr. Pintar would be able to call himself an Ironman. Tom was about to embark on a mission to fulfill his goal that he set for himself almost a year ago. He registered for Ironman Wisconsin on September 13th, 2004 and today was the day he would push himself both physically and mentally.

Anyone who endeavors to do an Ironman faces many obstacles along the journey toward the finish line, and like me, Tom had an additional obstacle. You see Tom is a diabetic.

I could go on and describe for you how over 2000 athletes entered the water at 6:30am anxiously waiting for the start of the race (2.4 mile swim), I could tell you about how the heat reached well over 98 degrees (I lost a couple of pounds myself that day), and how over 400 athletes did not finish the bike segment (112 miles) of the race, or I could tell you about how at one point during the run (26.2 miles) Tom became hypoglycemic and had to walk until his blood sugars levelled off. These are just a few of the obstacles that he faced that day.

I want to share with all of you a moment during the race that moved me. This one moment made a lasting impression and brought a smile to my face and tears to my eyes. Dr. Pintar had a wonderful support system with him on race day. His wife, his children, his parents, and I were all there cheering him on. His father, Tom Pintar Sr. was standing next to me as the race began. We both watched as over 2000 athletes began swimming. It was this moment that made a lasting impression. I turned my head and noticed as tears of pride filled Tom's father's eyes. It made me think of my mother who I had lost to lung cancer in January. I thought about how she must have felt, and wondered if those same tears filled her eyes as she sat in front of her computer on July 25th, 2004 watching Ironman live as I began a similar journey.

I remembered how sick she was, how the chemotherapy ravaged her body, and how she could not make it to Lake Placid to watch me compete. What I saw in Tom's father's eyes really affected me. How he stood there and watched his son, a diabetic, take on one of sports most gruelling events, hit close to my heart as I thought of my mother. In his father's eyes I saw Lake Placid again and I saw my mother sitting at her computer filled with cancer but determined to support her son. I saw the pride I knew she felt and it made me proud to be able to share that moment with his father.

To everyone in this chapter, who have been there for me through my toughest of times, and the ones I can now call some of my best, I thank you and want you to know how grateful I am for everything you have done.

The relationships I have built through my experiences over the years are ones that I will always hold close to me, and I can only hope that as time goes by, those relationships will strengthen and in addition, new ones will flourish.

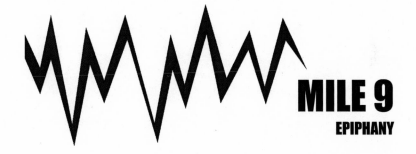

MILE 9

EPIPHANY

Years had passed and I recovered physically, but emotionally I was still in shattered pieces. My athletic dreams and a promise made faded into the blackness of anger. My body eventually stabilized and I regained my strength. I made it back to being just like every other dialysis patient. I suffered from muscle wasting, anaemia, dialysis fatigue, and other sorted issues. I was tolerating dialysis but had this immense feeling of panic. I felt like I was running out of time and the clock was ticking.

At night I was still terrified to go to sleep. I would dream that I was sixteen years old again, and I kept hearing the doctors' voices, "He is not expected to live past the age of twenty five." I was haunted nightly and confronted daily by the ghosts of decisions past.

For so many years I lived a self destructive, non-compliant life. I knew all along that the decisions I made were not the best ones, but I based those decisions on a life that I felt was worthless. The doctors said that I was going to die by the age of twenty-five so what was the point? I had dreams, not nightmares as a child. What happened?

I wanted to be an athlete and a lawyer, but by the time I turned sixteen I had given up. I wanted so much more out of life. The anger and blackness grew as I thought about everything and I began to curse God. I told him that it was not fair. I blamed him for everything as I sat in the middle of my living room floor and screamed, "Why am I still alive?" I broke down and began crying. After about fifteen minutes I picked myself off of the floor and went to the bathroom. I turned on the water and cupped some in my hands. I splashed it on my face and looked in the mirror. Who am I? What have I done with the past nine years of my life? I had more questions than answers, and I did not like who I had become. This was how I spent most of my 25th birthday.

My mother had a tradition on our birthdays. She would call and sing to each of us. My brother's birthday is April 30th and mine is May 27th. Both Sean and I used to laugh about the calls, but now both of us would give anything for one more of those birthday phone calls from our mother. She was not the best singer in the world but her singing voice was music to our ears.

The phone rang and I debated on whether or not I would answer it. I knew it was my mother. I picked it up and got a surprise. Both she and Bob were singing.

"Happy Birthday to you, Happy Birthday to..." A real Sonny and Cher act. I wiped the water from my face and smiled. They both finished singing and told me they loved me. We talked for a few minutes and I told my mother that I had something important to tell both her and Bob. She asked what it was, but I told her that I would talk about it with them at dinner. We made plans to meet at 7pm later that night. I had a big announcement and I knew that it would take some convincing in order to get them both to help me.

I walked in to the restaurant with nervous anticipation. My mind was racing. As I approached the table my parents smiled. "Happy Birthday" they said. I smiled, pulled out the chair, and sat down. My mother knew right away that something was on my mind. "What's wrong?" she asked. I had told her nothing, but she knew. She could always look in my eyes and tell right away. I never could keep anything from her. I started to tell them what was on my mind but the waitress approached and introduced herself "Hi, my name is Julie, and I am going to be your waitress today." I immediately responded, "Hi, that's Bob, that's Peg, and I'm Shad, well be your customers today." My mother kicked me under the table and with a sharp tone said my first and middle name, "Shad Richard." She was not pleased. The waitress laughed and said, "that was original." I liked her sarcasm and she was cute. We ordered our food and the waitress left. As she walked away she gave me a look and a smile. I knew she would give me her phone number all I had to do was ask. You know the business.

I looked at my parents and smiled, they smiled back and shook their heads. Now was the hard part. I had to ask my parents for their help again, so I began cautiously. I started to explain certain decisions in my life and why I made them. I asked my parents to help me. I told them I wanted to change my life. I told them that I needed to go to school. Bob asked "What do you want Shad?" His voice was always very straightforward so it made me nervous to ask. "Can I move back into your house by Lake Nokomis? I promise I will go to school." Both my parents looked at each other, waited a few seconds, and as usual my mother responded. "We will have to discuss it." I felt uneasy.

As we finished dinner I noticed all of the wait staff approaching. Julie our waitress was carrying a birthday cake. My parents had planned this before I arrived. Everyone in the restaurant began singing. I was embarrassed. When everyone finished singing Julie bent down and placed the cake in front of me. She winked and said "Happy Birthday." I smiled.

The rest of the night was filled with conversations of years past and lots of laughter. The events from earlier in the day were far from my mind. It was getting late and my parents had to work early the next morning so I gave them both a hug and thanked them for a great birthday. My mother held me extra tight and told me she loved me. This was a special birthday for her. I think she remembered what the doctors said.

I watched as my parents walked toward the door. I reached down, grabbed my coat, and walked toward the bar. I saw Julie waiting for her drink order. She smiled as I approached. I asked her if she had a minute. She did. We talked for a few minutes and I gave her my number. She said she would call me tomorrow. I left the restaurant feeling pretty good overall. As I walked through the parking lot I thought about everything that had happened that day. It had been long and emotionally I was drained.

I arrived home to a dark apartment. I opened the door and stood in the entryway for a moment, and noticed the red flashing light on the counter. I turned on the light and walked over to the counter. I pressed the button on my answering machine and the voice said "You have one new message." I smiled because I was sure it was Julie, but it wasn't. She never called. You know the business.

The voice on my answering machine was my mothers. She had called to tell me that she and Bob talked about me moving back into the house by Lake Nokomis. They decided that I could move in with two conditions. No parties and good grades. She stressed that they also wanted to see my class registration. "You can come out to the house and pick up the keys this weekend. Happy 25th Birthday; I love you." I was excited. I had thought they were going to say no for sure. Instead, the next day I would take the first of many difficult steps. That day I would register for college again and see if one more time I could start fresh and begin a new more positive life.

MILE 10
COLLEGE

I have attempted and failed at college many times. Over the years I realized that the reason I consistently failed was because I wasn't ready. College takes discipline and for most of my life I lacked that. I remember the first time I started college. I was sixteen and had registered for classes at the University Of Minnesota. I spent almost two years there and completed only one class before being kicked out. I guess I majored in dysfunction. I pledged a couple of fraternities, joined the crew team as a coxswain, and studied the art of keg standing. I wonder how different my life would have been if I had not found out that my life expectancy was so short.

It was only a month after classes had begun that I was given the news that I would not live past the age of twenty-five. I remember that night clearly, feeling numb, wanting to cry and wanting to scream. I made a life changing decision that night as I walked home after receiving the news. It was to be the first of many bad decisions in my life. I had given up and gave in to the darkness, spending the last six years fighting for my life and I had nothing left.

As I saw it, it was only a matter of time and the race for my life was over. I saw no point in pursuing my hopes and dreams because I would surely never make the finish line.

The next few weeks were filled with depression. I over slept my classes, and put a lot of money into the vending machines. I lived on chips, candy bars, and soda pop, everything a dialysis patient is not supposed to eat. At that point I didn't care. I spent all of my time sleeping and eating. I was waiting to die.

It was on a Saturday afternoon that my life would once again change directions. I still had a fatalistic view of my situation but after that Saturday I would at least have something to look forward to and something to occupy my time. I entered the poolroom in the basement of the dorm with the intention of playing pool but two guys were already playing. I walked over to the table and said that I had next game.

The two guys who were playing stopped and looked at me for a minute, smiled, and told me that the pool table was for students only. This pissed me off but I didn't realize how young I looked. At the time I stood five feet tall and weighed 90lbs. I told them that I was a student and that five dollars said I could beat both of them. They laughed and took my challenge. And that was how I met

Mike Elliott.

I took a deep breath and pulled the pool cue back. I had one shot left. "Eight ball, side pocket." It was a perfect cut. That black ball rolled into the woven leather pocket as the cue ball rolled and stopped short of the corner hole. I looked at Elliot and smiled. "That will be five dollars each" I said. His friend, who was his fraternity brother, gave me five dollars and said good game. Elliot told me that he did not have any cash on him and that he needed to go back to his room to get it so I followed him back. When we got there he introduced me to his roommate, and that was how I met Dan.

I would stop by to see if Elliot was around sometimes and Dan would be there, studying. He and I would sit and talk about sports, school, and some of the girls on campus. We developed a friendship that has lasted over the years.

Elliot paid me the five dollars and gave me a flyer to a party. He asked me if I liked to dance and I told him I did. He told me that the party started at 9pm that night, there was a five-dollar cover charge and that they would have three different DJ'S spinning. "This is going to be the biggest party of the year." I read the flyer and asked him what a Sigma party was. He just laughed.

Mike Elliot was a Sigma. They were an African American fraternity on campus. He told me about the Sigmas and asked if I was still coming to the party. "You will probably be one of the only white guys there." Then he asked if that would bother me. I told him not at all. I turned to leave and said, "I will see you at the party."

Elliot was working the door to the party. He noticed me right away and let me circumvent the line. I walked in and could not believe all the people. The music was loud and people were dancing everywhere. I noticed that people were standing around in a giant circle cheering, so I walked over to see what all the cheering was about. I watched as one by one, someone took their turn in the center of the circle; the energy was contagious. So I waited until the circle was empty and jumped right in. I had a great time at the party and made a few friends. I was hooked. It had started off innocently enough. Dancing became my passion and it was what I wanted to do with the rest of what I thought would be a short life. I wanted to party until the end. This was the first night I met the rabbit. I followed him down the hole and all the way to

Wonderland. From that night on all I wanted to do was party.

I thought about going back to the University of Minnesota, but because of those memories, decided against it. I knew it was disaster waiting to happen, and this time my better judgement won out. Before going to my parent's house to pick up the keys I needed to register for classes so I gathered my records and made an appointment with the counselor at Metropolitan State University. I went through the meeting process, applied and was accepted. I registered for classes and moved back into Bob's house by Lake Nokomis.

The first class I registered for was a philosophy course. I initially feared this class but it turned out to be one that I enjoyed and one that changed my life. I believe that in our lives we are all faced with pivotal moments; moments when we are confronted by our actions and offered a choice to change. These choices can lead to major changes in our lives and this philosophy class was one of those times when I was given a choice. I had taken the first step by going back to college, and by registering for this class I had taken one more step in the right direction. At the time I didn't know it, but this class would have a major impact on my future.

The first day back to college was pretty easy. I only had one class scheduled. It was this Philosophy class. I didn't know what to expect and was worried about the workload, but off I went. I found the classroom and took my seat. The professor walked in and introduced himself. Each of us was required to stand up and do the same. After everyone did, the professor told the class to pick up a pen and a piece of paper. He wanted each of us to write about a traumatic experience in our lives. I laughed out loud and he called on me. "What seems to be so funny Mr. Ireland?" I told the professor that my entire life had been traumatic. He responded by saying, "I guess you have a lot to write about then don't you." I nodded my head and picked up my pen. The words began to flow and so did the tears.

Over the course of the next fifteen weeks I spent a lot of time reading and writing. This was the professor that gave me "Tuesdays with Morrie" to read. He was the professor who challenged me to ask questions and seek answers. He was the one who asked me if I thought education was a gift. Throughout the entire course he taught us the three tools that I would later use to change my life. These tools, **Reflection**, **Realization**, and **Perception** were the fundamental building blocks for the **Deal, Accept, Live** process that I later developed.

Life is a series of moments comprised of choices. With each choice comes the opportunity to change your life. Over the course of my life I have watched several of these moments and choices pass me by. Fear and anger ruled everything I did and that led me to make the wrong choices.

During that fifteen-week class I was given the tools that helped me to understand the origin of my fear and how to embrace my anger. I was given the tools to make better choices. Over the course of this fifteen-week class I took the first step and asked myself the hard questions and sought answers. I reconnected with hope and took physical action. I accepted the challenges in my life and learned to live with the things I could not change. For the first time I felt like I was in control.

I spent a few years at Metropolitan State University and am currently a few credits short of graduating. During my sophomore year I changed majors and co-enrolled in Dakota County Technical College. I decided to pursue a technology career that would take me on a shorter educational career path.

The technology market was exploding and I wanted to take advantage of the financial opportunities that were available. The program I graduated from was a six-month MCSE (Microsoft Certified Systems Engineer) course and then I entered the technology market at the height of its explosion. I was genuinely beginning to feel successful, and finally started to realize that I could accomplish the things in life I wanted to, if I'd just give them a chance.

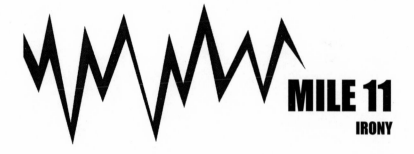

MILE 11

IRONY

I entered the technology market with three job offers so my services went to the highest bidder. I couldn't wait to start making the professional wages we were promised in school. I didn't realize that when people pay you professional wages you are expected to provide professional services. I worked twelve-hour shifts and struggled for the first two weeks, but I adapted and settled into my routine. My first job was on a major roll out project for one of the largest financial service providers. We worked from 5pm until 5am. I hated the shift but the money was unbelievable. After the first month I started to realize that all I ever did was work. I did what I was told, got an education, made great money, yet I was still unhappy. I didn't understand why I felt this way. I liked what I was doing, but I missed the point completely. I had gone into technology for all of the wrong reasons, and it would take almost two years before I realized it.

The problem with project work was the duration of the projects. Most of the time they were short term and usually completed ahead of schedule which left everyone but the project managers competing for new project assignments. Add to that the technology markets volatility after Y2K and I was left with a lot of instability. The job market cooled off and I found myself competing for jobs that paid about half of what I was making before. I was going on interviews and talking to placement agencies. The competition was tough and initially my enthusiasm during the interview process worked against me.

One day, I walked into a hiring manager's office nervously confident. I sat down and waited for him to finish his phone call. After a couple of minutes he hung up, leaned back in his chair, and asked me to tell him about myself. So I started to tell him about my work experience, my education, and some of my personal interests. He sat in his chair and listened intently. I told him why he should hire me and what I could do for the company. He was smiling and things were going well. The answer to his next question definitely shocked him. He was not expecting my response and it was not until a few days later that I would realize the error I made. "Tell me Shad, where do you see yourself in the next six months?" I looked him straight in the eyes and responded, "In your chair." He was not amused. I thought the answer showed an eagerness to work; that I was dedicated to working hard and interested in advancement. He did not see it that way. He quickly terminated the interview. I learned to curtail my enthusiasm in the interviews that followed but found that I didn't have the years of experience to compete with everyone else. I ended up taking a help desk position to gain experience.

I went to work for one of the largest companies in technology. They provided a multitude of services and one of those was technical support/help desk. I was excited to be working for this company because of the potential for advancement. I came into the position with a solid background and hit the ground running. I was given first shift to accommodate my medical needs and settled into my daily routine. I would go to work form 6am until 2pm then head to dialysis. After a couple of weeks the novelty of the position wore off and I was back to feeling generally unhappy.

In between phone calls I would sit and daydream while other guys I worked with would sit and read all the latest technology magazines. They loved it, while I looked at it as a job and simply a paycheck. This was when I started to realize that my reasoning for choosing a career in technology made no sense and I had made a mistake. I asked myself the question that needed to be asked, and found that I didn't like the answer. I was not pursuing my goals and dreams. I was in technology for the money and it made me unhappy. In the middle of that thought the chime in my headphone rang which meant I had an incoming call. The person on the other end of the phone was about to change my life.

"Thank you for calling the help desk, this is Shad, how can I help you?" The person on the other end of the line was from the University. "Mr. Ireland, we have a kidney in route. You need to come to the hospital. Station 5C." I was shocked and excited. I was going to get another chance at a kidney transplant.

As I rushed to the hospital I started to have reservations. I flashed back to an earlier time when I was in the hospital fighting through rejection episodes. I thought about the weird side effects I experienced to the immune suppressive medication. I thought about how I almost lost my life. These things scared me and gave me cause to question the decision I was about to make. Then I thought about my goals and dreams. I thought about Europe and the choices I watched pass me by. I thought about dialysis and how I would have given anything for a chance at a normal life again. When I got to the hospital I was not as excited.

I saw one of the nurses I knew and asked her a few questions. She reminded me of the fact that it had been years since my first kidney transplant and that new drugs were being used along with different transplant protocols. So I walked down the hallway and took a seat in the waiting area. I knew the routine and figured it was going to be another long night.

The surgery went extremely well and I awoke to the same pain I felt after my first transplant. The problem was that the kidney was not working. The transplant doctors told me that this was not unusual. Sometimes the kidney needed time to adjust. This was called ATN. The kidney was in shock. I was told it could take anywhere from a week up to two months before the kidney could begin to function. I was worried, and what really scared me was that I began to have the same symptoms as before. My body began reacting to the immune suppressive medications and I felt like I was on the same slippery slope again. The phone rang and I reached over to answer it. "Hello" I said. It was my Manager calling from work. He made small talk for a few minutes then got down to business. He told me that if I was not able to come back to work on Monday that he would have to fill my position. He gave me some song and dance about our contract to the client, and how our SLA'S (Service Level Agreements) were falling behind due to my absence. He told me the call volume was increasing over the last month BLAH, BLAH, BLAH. The bottom line was that I was being let go. I was panicked. I began to worry about my bills and what little I had in savings. I became angry and afraid and wondered what I was going to do now. Earlier that day I was told that I was being discharged but not cleared to go back to work. I needed to go home and rest. I sat in my hospital room and cried, watching as the darkness started to close in again.

I of course lost my job and the mandatory rest period turned into two months of waiting. The kidney was not working. My body was reacting the same way it had previously reacted to the first transplant and I was desperate and afraid.

I could see that my body was deteriorating again and was convinced that if they didn't take this kidney out I would be dead in less than two months. I had multiple symptoms yet the doctors were still optimistic. Even though the kidney had no function they wanted me to wait at least six months before they would consider removing the transplant. Meanwhile I was unable to work and had no idea how I was going to support myself. My savings were almost depleted. Fear and anger came roaring back. I made a decision to seek another opinion. I wanted the transplanted kidney removed.

It had been over two months with no signs of it ever going to work. I tried to discuss everything with the transplant team but was told that if I proceeded I would never receive another kidney again. I would be on dialysis for the rest of my life and no one would ever transplant me. I was quite upset after this conversation and felt like I had no options. I am the type of person who comes out swinging when I am backed into a corner, so I found another team of doctors who agreed to remove the transplanted kidney under one condition. I had to give the kidney at least one more month to begin to function. I agreed and hoped that the kidney would show some sign of life. It never worked and so the kidney was removed.

I sat in the hospital for a week after surgery feeling very depressed. My life was in pieces again. My body had significantly deteriorated since receiving the second kidney, I had lost my job, burned through all of my savings, and I was now considered ineligible for another kidney transplant because of the decision I had made. At that moment suicide entered the room and poured me another drink but I picked up the glass and poured it on the floor. I'd had a moment of clarity. I went back in my mind to the philosophy class I took, and everything I'd learned. It all made perfect sense. I knew what I needed to do.

I had to embrace the one thing I could never embrace and start to take control. I took physical action and chose to embrace dialysis. This was something I couldn't change so I had to focus on getting stronger. I examined the last few months and came to the conclusion that my body would not accept the immune suppressive medications. The side effects had left me in a debilitated state. Even though they had told me I was ineligible for another kidney transplant I told myself that I was going to make the decision. It was about control, so I took it. **I chose** to never take another transplant. That decision left me standing face to face with the monster. That was my perception and **it** needed to change too. I began to research dialysis and its effects, looked at different protocols in different countries. I read about home dialysis in Canada and longer dialysis treatments in Europe. I asked the questions, and sought out the answers, and developed an overall plan of action. I believed that dialysis and its effects on the body could be controlled, so as I continued to do research I became excited about the possibilities.

It took me six months to recover from the debilitating affects of the second transplant. I struggled emotionally. There were days that I would feel positive about my progress, and days that I would sit alone at home and drink alcohol until I passed out. I eventually transferred to another dialysis clinic and found a great Nephrologist.

I continued to do research and approached my doctor on a monthly basis. I would tell him about the studies I'd read about and the different things going on in dialysis around the world. I'm not sure what my doctor thought at the time, but he indulged my requests. We increased my dialysis treatment time to four hours three times a week, increased the size of the artificial kidney used during dialysis, switched to 14 gauge needles, and increased my dialysis treatment blood flow to 600 a minute.

What I'd read about and researched came true. We watched as my laboratory results improved. I stared to feel better and became stable. These positive results only fed my hunger to learn more. I wanted to perfect the dialysis treatment process. The next request I had was turned down due to how the dialysis reimbursement system is set up in this country. I'd approached my doctor with the idea to add an extra dialysis treatment a week. He explained to me that my lab results were too good. I tried to explain to him that I still suffered from dialysis fatigue, had little muscle strength (due to muscle wasting) and other symptoms. He responded by telling me that I was well above the KDOQI adequacy recommendations. 70% was the standard. I did more research and learned about EPO. The following month I asked my doctor to increase my EPO dose. I explained to him about what I'd read and why I felt that it should be increased. Dialysis patients suffer from anemia and the EPO I was receiving was not adequately providing the energy I needed to meet my daily physical needs. The KDOQI guidelines and the reimbursement protocols called for a patient's hemoglobin to be kept between 11 and 12. Normal hemoglobin for a male, non-dialysis patient is between 13.3 and 15.3. I couldn't function at this level. I researched the Medicare guidelines and came across the medical exception order. (Thank God for this provision) I came back to my doctor and told him that I had symptoms which made it difficult for me to function at the stated reimbursement guidelines. He was not aware of the medical exception order and did some research of his own. Fortunately for me my doctor did the research and was open minded. He increased my EPO dose and raised my hemoglobin to no greater than 13. In all fairness I understand that EPO is an expensive drug, and that studies have shown that increasing EPO alone does not have a direct clinical effect, but when combined with exercise and physical activity the patient is able to lead a more productive life. (Patients are able to work, pay taxes, interact with their families, etc...)

If the powers that be would take a macro perspective approach to the problem they would realize and come to the same conclusion I have.

The current approach to reimbursement (still using 1978 standards) and the overall treatment of dialysis patients in this country is minimal at best. In this country we have the ability to provide better affordable care yet we choose not to under the disguise of cost management. I would challenge those in positions of authority to re-examine the reimbursement model and look at the overall picture.

We are spending and wasting more under the current model! I read an article that quoted the following numbers, 5% of the Medicare budget goes to ESRD (End Stage Renal Disease) in this country. (USA) Of that 5%, 41% is spent on hospitalizations. Those numbers are quite staggering. This disease is dollar intensive and we are facing a medical crisis in this country. This means that we are faced with a choice. We can invest those dollars on the front end and implement what I would call **The Patient Quality of Life Model** (preventative medicine) or continue to invest those dollars on the backend treating complications and other correlating diseases as they develop.

I would challenge everyone who reads this to do as I have. Ask questions and seek answers. The conclusion I have come to, and **The Patient Quality of Life Model** I have developed, if implemented across the board, has the potential to save the Medicare system millions to hundreds of millions of dollars. This model also creates an improvement in the patient's overall quality of life so everyone wins. This idea for **The Patient Quality of Life Model** helped to inspire me to create the Shad Ireland Foundation. Although in its infancy, the success my foundation is having with patients is remarkable. I believe that in time, the foundation will have enough data to substantiate **The Patient Quality of Life Model** hypothesis.

As I continued to work with my doctor, and pushed for better treatment outcomes, I came to the conclusion that physical fitness could possibly counteract the effects of dialysis so I decided to test this idea and purchased a gym membership. I have to tell you that I struggled and felt quite embarrassed with my physical condition at the beginning.

Due to my increased EPO dose I had more energy, but still suffered from muscle wasting. I spoke with my doctor about the struggles I was having in the gym, so he drew a few lab tests and suggested that we try a drug called Carnitor. (currently available for limited use in the USA) The results I had after taking this drug (combined with physical activity and nutrition) were impressive. Over the next sixty days I was able to increase muscle and directly counteract the issue of muscle wasting. I personally believe that Carnitor should be an option for doctors to use to address this issue in dialysis patients. I would like to see it used (in a study) in combination with the fitness grant program my foundation provides to patients. I believe that study would show similar results. Again I would challenge the powers that be to re-examine the issues of access to treatments such as these and study the potential benefit of **The Patient Quality of Life Model** I have developed.

Over time my physical and emotional outlook improved as I stabilized and became well adjusted to life on dialysis. I worked with my doctor and took a more active role in my care. Working together, we were able to individualize my treatment plan and perfect the dialysis outcomes. As I did more research I discovered a type of treatment called home hemo-dialysis. At the time I was told that this type of treatment option was not available to patients in the USA. I talked with my doctor and shared with him my ideas about every other day dialysis. Little did I know that this type of treatment would be an option for patients in the not too distant future. I used to dream about home dialysis and the freedom it would provide. That dream came true for me and it is the way that I currently receive my dialysis treatments.

I receive dialysis four days a week for 4.5 hours per treatment. We use an every other day rotating schedule to ensure stable and adequate dialysis which has garnered amazing results. The reason I have been able to have the success I've had is because of my dialysis team. My doctor and the home dialysis program I participate in communicate, and work together to continually improve my outcomes. We have taken a more individualized approach and have really perfected the process. **(Thank you Don, Brian, Linda, Theresa, Angie and everyone else involved in the Minneapolis/St. Paul home program)**

I eventually felt well enough to try and find a full time job again so I went back to what I knew. I applied for and was hired as a Level 2 Help Desk Technician. I started working for a great company but we were sold. Life at the new company became unbearable after the initial honeymoon period wore off. They came to us saying that we were required to take a 50% pay cut or lose our job. Many of my co-workers quietly began seeking other employment opportunities. I should have also looked because a month later my position was officially phased out. I didn't see it coming. There I was unemployed again and disenfranchised with the entire technology market. I didn't know what I was going to do with myself. I only had a couple thousand dollars saved so I was stressed out and worried. What I did next surprised a lot of people, especially my mother, but it would wind up being another life changing experience.

I met Stacie a few months earlier and we had talked about me coming out to California sometime for a visit. I called her on the phone and told her that I was unemployed. I laughed about it and told her I needed a vacation. It was close to my birthday so I figured I deserved a nice gift this year. I booked my ticket and we made plans for my trip. Little did I know what life had in store for me. During this trip I was going to experience another moment of clarity. I boarded the plane and settled in for a three hour and forty-three minute plane ride. I sat back in my seat as the plane lifted off and thought about how nice it was going to be to go back to California. I pondered life and all of the choices and opportunities I now had.

I could have easily gotten depressed again but I chose not to. Life is about choice and perception, so I chose to look at the situation and consider the opportunities available to me. I chose not to consider what I'd lost, but rather, what I'd gained. I was going to focus on having a good time and, when I got back to Minnesota I would decide what I wanted to do next. I was in control.

My head jerked as the plane touched down in California. I'd just nodded off as we began our decent. I tried to fall asleep throughout the entire flight, but my mind was troubled. I didn't know what I was going to do and it bothered me. As a matter of fact it stayed on my mind throughout most of my time in California. It would be an experience on the Third Street Promenade that would again facilitate change in my life.

Stacie and I had a great time and on the afternoon before I was scheduled to leave, she introduced me to a street vendor friend of hers. He had a small table with different types of items. We began talking strangely enough about the Law. After several minutes of ideological exchange he shook my hand and said to me that he respected my opinions and he wanted me to take a souvenir back to Minnesota so that I would remember the experience. I smiled and thanked him but he would not take no for an answer. I accepted his offer and looked down at the table. Immediately something caught my eye. I noticed a bumper sticker, and what initially caught my eye, was located in the center, on the bottom. It read Minneapolis MN 55076. Next I read the entire bumper sticker and began laughing out loud. I picked it up and told him I would take the bumper sticker. He smiled and winked at me. It was like he knew. You see, the entire trip I was worried about my future. I didn't know what I was going to do next. It was ironic to me that I had traveled to California and found the answer on a bumper sticker. It was one that had originated in Minneapolis MN and that seemed specifically meant for me. As I walked away Stacie came up along side of me and asked, "What was so funny? What did the bumper sticker say on it?"

I shook my head in disbelief and laughed again. I turned to Stacie and told her, "It says, Remember Who You Wanted to Be." She told me she didn't get it. "I don't see what is so funny" she said. I didn't try to explain it to her. The message was meant for me.

MILE 12

A PROMISE REMEMBERED

I arrived home from California with a new sense of enthusiasm and purpose. I spent the entire plane ride reflecting on my childhood. I thought about the hopes and dreams I had so many years ago, and about how I could make those childhood hopes and dreams a reality. I remembered who I wanted to be.

I felt like a child on the night before Christmas, filled with excitement and anticipation. I couldn't wait to tear into my future. As I walked through the airport, I again went back to the philosophy class I took at Metropolitan State and reflected on my current situation. I was never really excited about a career in technology. I had always looked at it as being just a job. I realized I was not happy, I was still living a life devoid of hopes and dreams, so I took action. I chose to perceive my situation in a positive light, and it made all the difference. Then it was easy to make the decision to finish my education. I was going to finally complete my undergraduate degree and apply to law school. As a child I had dreams of being an athlete and then graduating from law school. I wasn't sure how I could ever fulfill the athlete part, given my condition, but I knew I could go back to Metropolitan State and finish my undergraduate degree. Getting accepted into law school was at least attainable if I really applied myself.

As I was leaving the airport my cell phone rang. "Speak," I said. The voice on the other end came back with a familiar "Sup." It was Troy. He had called to wish me a Happy Birthday. He asked me if I had plans, and I told him not really, so he insisted that I meet him and Chris for a few drinks. Chris was Troy's girlfriend at the time.

We went out and celebrated my birthday, and ended up having more than a few drinks. It felt good to hang out with both of them again. It had been awhile since I went out with my friends and we made up for lost time. We stopped by a few clubs, danced, and went shot for shot. I looked at my watch and realized it was getting late. Troy put his arm on my shoulder and said "Time flies when you're drinking; I missed you bro, Happy Birthday." We had been drinking for several hours. I was drunk and hungry, so I asked Troy and Chris if they wanted to leave and get something to eat. They agreed, so we left for Perkins.

Perkins was the place to go after a night of drinking. We had spent many a drunken evening there socializing. Even though I had not been back in Wonderland for year's things hadn't changed. We still saw the same people at the clubs, and everyone still went to

Perkins afterward.

As we sat in the booth waiting to order we talked about old times, joked and reminisced. I laughed with Troy and Chris but my mind was in another place.

I was thinking about my trip to California and the bumper sticker I was given. I was thinking about law school and remembering who I wanted to be. I snapped back into reality when Troy and Chris started talking about when I lost my first transplant. They talked about the 75lb man I used to be and how much I had changed. "You have come along way bro," Troy said. I nodded my head, "Yeah I have" I responded. The mood became somber and silence set in. I sat there in a state of retrospective remembrance. The floodgates opened and I was swept away by the memories. I was back, sitting in that shower, then moments later, lying on my mothers couch. I was 75lbs again and being washed away by emotions as I struggled to swim for the shore. I was drowning in the memory of it all, and the fact that I was drunk didn't help. Tears began forming in my eyes as I saw myself lying on my mothers couch watching TV. I was having an out of body experience, watching my former self. I turned my head to see what was on the TV and that was it. I suddenly came rushing back to reality, and found my self back in the moment. I had a blank look on my face and both Troy and Chris asked me if I was all right. I must have looked comatose. I had so many things rushing through my mind I couldn't speak. I was debating whether or not I would tell them what I just saw and remembered. Then I had a moment of clarity; it all finally made sense. Losing my job, the trip to California, the bumper sticker, my thoughts as I walked through the airport in Minnesota. I remembered who I wanted to be. It was at that moment I was given a choice, and took the opportunity, so I blurted it out, "I am going to compete in the Ironman World Championship."

A few moments of silence were followed by laughter. I was stunned. Did they not understand the significance of this moment? I tried in vain to explain myself but looking back, I can now understand their response. I sat across the table from both of them with a cigarette in one hand and a cup of coffee in the other. "I made a promise to myself. I am going to be an Ironman. I remembered who I wanted to be." I was rambling. We had been doing a lot of drinking.

Troy and Chris decided to try and talk some sense into me. "Shad, there is no way. You have been on dialysis for over twenty years.

Do you even know what an Ironman is?" With each comment I became angrier because I couldn't make them understand. Ever since my diagnosis I felt like I was slowly drowning in a sea of emotional uncertainty. Giant waves of fear and anger constantly crashed over my head as happiness always loomed on the horizon. Over the past few years I had learned to swim better but it still felt like I was treading water. I embraced that promise like a life raft.

The next morning I awoke to a raging headache and the memory of a promise made. As I sat up in bed a giant smile came across my face. I thought to myself, I need to register for the Ironman World Championship race right away, so I logged on to the Internet and spent the day educating myself.

I was naïve. I honestly thought that I would just pay the entry fee, register, train, and show up on race day. How hard could it be? I knew how to swim, bike and run. But as I did my research I read about the history of Ironman and how athletes "Got to Kona". Basically you had to earn it. You were either invited or you qualified. I looked at all the races and picked one. Again I was very naïve. I chose Lake Placid because of its history. I had no idea that Lake Placid was one of the toughest Ironman courses. I made a list of things to do and headed off to dialysis.

I was very fortunate to have had doctors who were so understanding and willing to work with me. I arrived at dialysis filled with excitement. I felt like I should get their approval before I started training, and to be honest, I was a little afraid of the entire undertaking. After about an hour of being connected to the machine my doctor approached and pulled up a chair. "How are you feeling today?" he asked. I told him I was feeling great, and immediately started rambling on about how I was going to do the Ironman in Lake Placid. I am sure he was surprised by my announcement. I asked him if being on dialysis would keep me from competing. "Can I do this?" I asked. He told me that he could not think of any medical reason that would keep me from my goal. "Go for it" he said. However he did tell me that most endurance athletes' potassium tended to trend high and that this might create a problem for me. "We should increase your dialysis treatment time to four hours and thirty minutes and keep an eye on your labs every week." That was all I needed to hear. I began training the next day.

What I didn't know was that my doctor was a marathoner. He understood the insanity that went into endurance sports. He was as excited about it as I was because to his knowledge it had never been done before. We both did research and found out that in fact it had never even been attempted because the medical consensus was that it couldn't be done.

Initially, the training was incredibly tough and I learned through trial and error. I read whatever I could on the Internet and talked with the personal trainers at the gym. I worked closely with my dietician to develop a special nutritional program because as a dialysis patient I couldn't follow the usual triathlete diet.

After the first thirty days I began to notice an overall improvement. I quickly came to the realization that fitness could counteract the effects of dialysis. A year later, this realization would help me to launch the Shad Ireland Foundation and create The Peg Smythe Fitness Grant program. It was the catalyst for the entire thing. I would later refer to what I was doing as an experiment. I wanted to again push the envelope and see how far we could take it. As I grew stronger, and my body developed, I became more confident. I was training everyday. All I did was go to my classes, the gym, and dialysis. I was truly happy for the first time in my life.

Six months into the training I felt unstoppable. I looked at my body and could not believe the muscular development. I was training all the time and honestly felt that I was going to go to Lake Placid and qualify for the World Championship race. Clearly I was still naïve.

I met Jared and Dan at the Lifetime Fitness gym. With out their help I would not have been able to accomplish what I did. I had heard from a friend of mine that they would be teaching a triathlon class and that they were both experienced Ironman triathletes. I walked up and introduced myself after class. Both Dan and Jared took a few minutes and asked me a series of questions. They seemed surprised to hear that I was a dialysis patient. "You don't look like a dialysis patient" they said.

People who compete at the Ironman level like challenges and I believe that Jared and Dan began coaching me for that reason. In a mater of six months they perfected my technique and improved my overall athletic ability. They gave me the tools and the encouragement to compete and I greatly improved as an athlete under their instruction.

138

I received a phone call one afternoon that devastated my existence. I was left feeling numb and wanting to escape. You can never prepare yourself for news like this. "I have cancer and it is terminal" my mother said. I dropped the phone. I arrived at my parent's house twenty minutes later. My mother sat there looking rather stoic. I gave her a giant hug like it was the last time I would ever see her.

She explained everything to me and gave me the truth. I looked at Bob and could only imagine what he was going through. My mother was diagnosed with small cell lung cancer with metastasis to the brain. This was a terminal diagnosis. She told me that they gave her four to twelve weeks to live. I was in shock. I told her to get a second opinion. I recently was given Lance Armstrong's book and was currently reading about his fight with cancer. I told my mom about Lance and what I had read. She told me she really liked her doctors but went and got a second opinion. They told her the same thing. I didn't know what to do. I felt helpless. My mother had been through so much in her life and she didn't deserve this. No one ever does. I wanted to take the cancer for her. She was now living the life she dreamed of so many years ago when she was alone with just her books. Now cancer was going to take that away. She had a loving and caring marriage with an amazing man who would be right there with her until her last breath. I held her hand tightly and told her to fight. I gave her a hug and told her I loved her. "You can beat cancer mom, Lance did." I read his book multiple times while I trained for Ironman Lake Placid and watched as my mother continued to deteriorate. His book became a personal source of comfort and hope.

When I first told my mother and father that I was going to do the Ironman they were in shock. My mother was a nurse and she believed that it could not be done. Both of my parents thought I was going to kill myself and of course they worried because they knew how stubborn I was.

"I was either going to cross the finish line or drop" I told them both. My mother believed, as did the majority of the medical community that it could not be done, but she knew better than to argue with me. Ever since I was little I would make up my mind to do something and that was it.

The doctors told my mother that there was no treatment for her Cancer but that if she wanted to try chemotherapy they would give it to her. My mother chose to take chemotherapy. I think her reasoning was because of us. I will not go into details about my mothers suffering or how I had to watch her deteriorate. It's still too painful for me. At the time I felt helpless and didn't know how to deal with the situation. I was angry. I'm still angry, and miss her so much. In the past I would have headed for the first drug or bottle I could find after receiving this kind of news. Instead I turned to training for comfort. I found redemption in the pain. The more my legs hurt the more I trained. It helped to ease my mind. As the weeks went by my mother had good days and bad. Before long six months had passed. Even though the chemotherapy was making her deathly ill I told her to keep fighting. I thought it was working, and she would beat the odds.

A few weeks before I would leave for Lake Placid I came to visit her. I told my mother that I wished she could be there to see me cross the finish line. She smiled and told me she would always be with me in spirit. I told her that I would make her proud. She kissed me and told me that she was already very proud of me. And with all that we had been through together, I knew she meant it with all her heart.

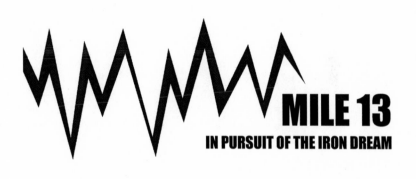

MILE 13

IN PURSUIT OF THE IRON DREAM

I arrived at Lake Placid with the intention of qualifying for the Ironman World Championship in Kona Hawaii. I had spent the entire year training, and was in the best shape of my life. I weighed 142lbs with 6% body fat. I felt ready but I was still very naïve. For me it had always been about a promise made; one event, one pursuit, the Iron Dream. When it was all said and done I would come to understand and realize that this was about so much more.

The training had been a constant companion for the past twelve months. We developed quite a friendship. I can't tell you how many times we shared the cold, wet rain on our long bike rides, and how many bitter winter mornings we ran outside before heading off to the pool. It was during these times that our friendship taught me what it would take to finish an Ironman.

Over the course of the training year I built my first website. I was amazed by the transformation of my mind and body. I developed ideas that turned into beliefs, and I wanted to share what I learned with other dialysis patients; *Physical fitness combined with proper nutrition can counteract the effects of dialysis.*

I received thousands of hits to my website and just as many emails. I found that other patients were as excited as I was. The emails came from patients, doctors, nurses, dieticians, and social workers from all around the world. Everyone shared their story and offered words of encouragement. They asked a lot of questions and wanted to know how they could have the same results. I also received emails from people who had other illnesses and faced different challenges. I was especially moved by one of those emails. I could relate to what was written because I remembered feeling the same type of hopeless desperation. In his email, Paul told me about his diagnosis. How at age thirty his life was falling apart. He was told that he had ALS and shared with me how alone he felt, and how he contemplated suicide. He had recently lost his job and the girlfriend whom he loved left him after hearing the news. He told me that he needed a friend and asked me for advice. I wasn't sure what to say so I prayed, and asked God to give me the wisdom to respond. In my response I told him that God loved him, and that he only gives us what we can handle. I shared with him how I'd also lost a woman who I truly loved because she was afraid of my diagnosis. I shared with him my experiences in college and the tools I learned. I told him about the book, "Tuesday's with Morrie" and the impact it had on me.

In closing, I told him to pursue his goals and dreams and that he would find happiness and fulfillment in those pursuits just as I have.

I looked at the overwhelming response to my website and what I was trying to accomplish and realized that what I was doing offered hope and inspiration to others. It was that realization that helped me to start to understand the meaning of it all.

I arrived at Lake Placid a week before the event. It is a small beautiful town steeped in American history. I couldn't believe I was there. Twenty-five hundred athletes came to participate in the Ironman and thousands more came as spectators. I walked around town and quietly watched all of the action. Athletes spent the week before the race swimming, riding, and running the course. I did the same. It was a few days before the race that I met the doctor who would write the orders for my dialysis treatments while I was there. This doctor was not a supporter. He made that quite clear at our first meeting. He walked into the examination room with a scowl on his face, looked over my orders, and bluntly stated the he was not pleased. He told me that if he'd known that I was coming to Lake Placid to compete in the Ironman he would have refused to provide dialysis. "What you are attempting is stupid. You are going to kill yourself. No dialysis patient can finish an Ironman" he said. I quietly smiled and kept the rage I felt inside because I needed him to sign my dialysis orders.

I was upset by this doctor's response but was not surprised. For every four positive emails I received, I would also receive one negative email. I had heard it all before, how I would not be able to finish the race, how I was going to kill myself, etc. It was frustrating to hear but I was confident in my training and my medical team supported my efforts.

I awoke on race morning with my stomach in knots. I felt like throwing up. I was extremely nervous and worried about the day ahead. I was confident in my training but in the back of my mind I kept hearing the words, "No dialysis patient can finish an Ironman."

I went to the staging area to get my race numbers inked on my arms and on the back of my calves. You could feel the nervous energy swirling in the air. My teeth chattered because it was a cool crisp morning. I went by and checked my bike before heading toward Mirror Lake. Everything looked good. I looked at my watch and it said 6:00 AM. I had one hour before the race started.

At 6:30 AM I put on my wetsuit and began to stretch. The swim transition area was starting to fill with other athletes. By 6:45 AM the area was completely full and athletes began entering the water. This was it. I felt like I could not breathe. I looked around as the family and friends of other athletes gave them hugs and words of encouragement. I thought about my family and friends. I wished all of them could have been there; my mother especially. I had come to Lake Placid by myself and to be honest, I was afraid.

With only a few minutes until the race began I walked slowly into the lake. I swam toward the far back and to the right. This was where all of the other first timers were located. I looked around at all of the people. There were bodies treading water everywhere. The coolness of the water helped to alleviate the tension in my muscles. 15, 14, 13, 12... The canon sounded and the race was underway. I was surrounded by mass chaos. I was getting kicked and hit as the other athletes who surrounded me began swimming.

The swim seemed to take forever. It was a two-loop course in which the athletes have only two hours and twenty minutes to finish 2.4 miles. In the water I had no concept of time.

As I approached the swim exit I was sure that I was close to the two-hour mark. When I exited the water I was quite surprised to see the official time clock. My official swim time with transition was 1:20:12.

The transition to the bike went extremely smooth. I came down the first hill feeling really strong and confident. Unfortunately, those feelings wouldn't last. What I didn't know was that I had thrown my back out during the swim. This was the first time I had used my wetsuit and the adrenaline was masking the pain. By mile sixty I was in tears. I could not keep proper form on the bike and the miles started to drag. I had to stop at one of the aid stations and try to find some Tylenol. One of the volunteers had Advil with her and gave me a couple.

I had to motivate myself to get back on the bike. This was the first time I wanted to quit. I thought about all of the patients from around the world who emailed me. I thought about my mom. I even thought about the doctor in Lake Placid who said I would fail. I told myself that the Advil would kick in within thirty minutes and all I had to do was hang in there. I climbed back on the bike and began to ride again. It was not until mile ninety before the Advil made the pain tolerable.

As I dismounted my bike and entered the transition area I was afraid to look at the official clock. I just finished 112 miles and my back was throbbing, my legs hurt, and my feet were numb. I hobbled toward the changing tent and glimpsed at the clock. It said that my official bike time was 8:13:48. I was disappointed with myself. I felt that I could have done better.

It felt good to sit down and put on my running shoes. I didn't want to get up but I pushed myself. I was no longer naïve. I had finally realized what exactly it would take to qualify for the Ironman World Championship race. I realized now that I needed to focus on finishing. I told myself, only 26.2 miles left.

I left the bike to run transition area and headed out onto the course. My legs felt like rubber and I could not feel my feet. My back was killing me but the Advil was making things tolerable. I was having a great day.

It was at mile one when things became difficult. The Advil wore off and I had this shooting pain that came from my left leg, up through my back, and into my neck. I could not run. Every step became more painful than the next. I was in bad shape and I new it. I kept telling myself the pain is only temporary.
I had 25.2 miles to go.

I struggled to run but the pain was excruciating. After a few more steps I accepted the fact that I would have to walk the rest of the way. It was starting to be a long day.

I watched as others ran by and shook my head in defeat. I felt alone. A voice called out "Hang in there Shad." I looked up to see who it was. It was another athlete on her way back into Lake Placid. I didn't know her, but her words brought a smile to my face. "You are looking strong" I responded. This is the essence of Ironman. We were all struggling together along this 140.6-mile journey. Time passed and eventually I became numb to the pain. It was pitch black and I was still a few miles from the finish line. I could see the lights and hear the crowd. I started to wonder if I was going to make it in time.

The Ironman consists of a 2.4-mile swim, a 112-mile bike ride, followed by a 26.2-mile run. Each event has a time limit, and the entire race needs to be completed within a 17-hour time frame. I felt like I had nothing left.
I had 2 miles to go.

I reached mile 25.2 and half smiled as fans cheered me on. At this point I was running on pure stubbornness and determination. As I walked the last mile, a volunteer who told me that he was there to make sure I made it in time approached me. His company was much needed and talking with him helped to keep my mind off of the pain. Before I knew it I was only a few blocks away from the finish line. I began to get excited.

I entered the Olympic sized oval feeling numb and drained. I really had to reach down deep to find the strength to finish and everything went into slow motion. Those last hundred yards seemed to take minutes. I tried to fight back the tears as I reflected back on my life. I thought about the seventy-five pound man I used to be and the promise I made to myself. I realized what I was about to accomplish and the impact it was going to have. With each painful step I began to pick up speed. When I saw the finish line I held my head up high and began to run.

I had thought about this moment all day and as I crossed the finish line the announcer's voice boomed. "Shad Ireland, you are an Ironman!" They placed the finishers medal around my neck and I was at a loss for words. My official time was 16:25:10.

On July 25th, 2004 I did what many said could not be done. I became the first dialysis patient to ever compete in and complete an Ironman triathlon. As I crossed that finish line I heard a voice say my name. I looked over my right shoulder and became surprised because I recognized who it was. He had traveled to Lake Placid in support of my pursuit of the Iron Dream. He waited all day for me to cross the finish line and when our eyes met we both smiled. The person I am talking about is that seventy-five pound man who spent thirteen months on his mothers couch. He mouthed the words "I am so proud of you" and faded into the crowd. Never to be seen again.

I was immediately taken to the medical tent for a mandatory check up. The entire medical team was sure that I needed to go to the hospital. I looked around the medical tent at all of the healthy athletes who were in worse shape than me. Many of them had IV'S and were waiting to go to the hospital. One of the local hospitals donated a portable lab facility for the race so they were able to draw my blood. Within minutes they had the results. We were all shocked when those results came back. The Doctor looked at me and then at the lab results. He told me that it did not make any sense. "You just completed a full Ironman and your lab results are normal (normal for a dialysis patient) he said. I just smiled. The doctor didn't know what to do so he kept me under observation for another half hour before letting me go. As I hobbled out of the medical tent, I took a deep breath and inhaled the night air. I held the finishers medal tightly against my chest and thought about how far I had traveled, and how far I had yet to go. As I slowly walked back toward my hotel I considered my options and began planning my next race. I still had a promise to fulfill.

My parent's car pulled up at the airport and I was surprised to see my mother in the passenger seat. She insisted that Bob bring her with him to the airport when they picked me up. I put my bags into the back of the SUV and jumped into the back seat. I had not seen my mother smile in seven months but today was different.

I took the finishers medal that hung around my neck and placed it over her head. I gave her a kiss on the cheek and hugged her tightly. I whispered in her ear "This medal is for you." She spent the next half hour on the phone calling her friends. She told everyone, "My son is an Ironman."

Over the next several months I watched as the cancer ravaged her body and she was reduced to a point of childlike helplessness. I watched as the man who thirteen years earlier promised to honor and cherish, in sickness and in health, did just that. My dad and my mother's friends, with the help of hospice, took care of her until the end. Her wish was to die at home surrounded by family and friends. The last two days of her life she spent in a coma. As I sat there holding her hand I thought about the six weeks that I spent in and out of a coma. I thought about how she sat there holding my hand, talking to me, so I did the same thing. I told her all the things I wanted to say. I told her all of my hopes and dreams. I talked about the Ironman in Hawaii, and promised her that we would one day cross that finish line together. Then I leaned over and kissed her on the cheek. I will never forget how cold she felt. I told her I loved her, and that it was ok to stop fighting. To my surprise she squeezed my hand and raised an eyebrow. I think it was her way of saying goodbye.

My mother was diagnosed with cancer on January 22nd 2004. She was given only one to three months to live. She died three hundred and sixty six days later at home surrounded by family and friends. She put her faith in Jesus and approached death like she lived her life, with dignity, faith, respect, courage, and compassion. Cancer tried to take my mother from me but she will always be with me because a thought is never far away. I love you mom.

MILE 14
OPPORTUNITY AND RESPONSIBILITY

We all have our own unique experiences and each one of these experiences contribute to the sum total of who we are. Individually, they comprise our own story, and within each individual story is a collective of universal emotions that make us brother and sister, that make us a community. We all experience those same universal emotions as we journey from initial diagnosis to the point of acceptance. As an adolescent and young adult, I spent many years living a life devoid of hopes and dreams. I was ruled by fear and anger and there were no role models; no one that I could see who was successfully living with kidney dialysis.

It was in my own unique experiences where I found the answers. It was there that I had to confront all of the pain in order to change. By embracing these experiences, as painful as they were, I was able to find acceptance and peace. It was this acceptance that helped me to perceive the world around me differently, and help me to transform into the Ironman triathlete I am today.

I have been asked many times how I was able to overcome twenty plus years of kidney dialysis in order to train for such an extreme event. The answer to that question is **individual inspiration**. I was inspired, and wanted to make a difference, not only in my life, but also in the lives of others who were facing the same struggles. I thought that if I could reach out and inspire one person then my athletic accomplishment would mean more than the realization of a personal dream. It would mean that I had made a difference. You see, I have been given an opportunity to be the role model I never had as a child, and I believe that I have a personal responsibility to give back to my community.

In other dialysis patients I see myself, and how I used to be. I recognize the daily struggle and the constant feeling of having no self-control. Isolation, anger, fear, and frustration can become overwhelming, but I know from personal experience that those feelings can change.

Reflection, **Realization**, and **Perception** were the tools I used to ask myself the questions and seek the answers. My goals, childhood dreams, and a promise I made to myself so many years ago inspired me to achieve what many believed could not be done. In my young life I have experienced so much. I have had great losses, but out of those losses I have achieved greater gains. My journey from the dialysis chair to the finish line has given me an understanding of what it means to be alive.

153

In training for and completing the Ironman at Lake Placid I have come to the understanding that it was never about the extreme distance or the external environment. It has always been about the inner struggle and those universal emotions we all face. All you can ever expect of yourself is that you gave everything you had when that moment came and you were faced with the ultimate challenge. It's not about the moment when you believe that you can't continue, it's about the moment after that as you reach down deep inside and find the strength to continue. To give up is easy, but turning life's obstacles into achievements and living the life you were given is the challenge. I have said many times, to live with a chronic illness is not a limitation but an invitation to those of us who are willing to accept the challenge. I have made it my responsibility to reach out to everyone that I can in the dialysis community and show them what's possible if you follow the philosophies and models I have laid out throughout this book. I have also made the most of my opportunity to prosper from all that I've learned on this journey. Here's your chance to now do the same. Make the most of it.

MILE 15
WHERE I'VE BEEN
WHAT I'VE DONE
AND WHAT IT ALL MEANS

Emotions, experiences, and connections make us all brothers and sisters. They make us a community. You see I was never alone. As the miles accumulated during the race for my life I learned to ask the questions and seek the answers. I guess I'm still doing that, but now those questions and answers are not as much for me, as they are for other brothers and sisters in our community who have yet to experience what I have. I want you all to see and come to understand what is possible and what I know to be true through my own personal experiences.

During the race for my life I have reflected on where I've been, realized what I've done, and experienced a positive change in my perception. Because I have learned to **Deal, Accept, Live** I am able to ask myself the ultimate question. What does it all mean? For me, at the stage of life I'm at now, the Ironman World Championship race in Kona Hawaii means another mile marker in my journey along the race that is my life.

Like the sport of triathlon, everyone approaches his or her own race personally. As much as we want others to race with us, that just can't be the case. Individually, the miles we must each travel varies. Some races are Sprints, others Olympic, while even more are Ironman.

I'm still in pursuit of the Iron Dream because of a promise made so many years ago. I will one day run with the best athletes in the world, and I wish everyone **NO LIMITATIONS ONLY INSPIRATION.**

Look for me in Kona.

'If I can reach out and inspire just one person then my athletic accomplishments will mean more than the realization of a personal dream, it will mean that I have made a difference."
Shad Ireland

SHAD IRELAND FOUNDATION

www.shadirelandfoundation.org

Helping patients to pursue their own finish line.

Q & A with Shad

Shad is available for appearances and speaking engagements. For more information please visit: **www.ironshad.com** or **www.shadirelandfoundation.org**